The Reading Solution

CHILDRENS' LITERATURE
and SERVICES

The Reading Solution

by Paul Kropp

RANDOM HOUSE

New York, Toronto, London, Sydney, Auckland

Published in 1993 by Random House of Canada Limited.

CANADIAN CATALOGUING IN PUBLICATION DATA
Kropp, Paul, 1948-
    The reading solution
    ISBN 0-394-22266-0
    1. Reading – Parent participation. 2. Literacy.
    I. Title.
    LC149.K76 1993   649'.58   C92-095492-8

With thanks to those authors, publishers and copyright owners for their kind permission to use extended quotations from copyrighted works:

From *Impressions*, © 1984. Reprinted by permission of Holt, Rinehart & Winston Ltd.

From *Our Daughter Learns to Read and Write* by Marcia Baghban, © 1984 The International Reading Association. Reprinted by permission of the author and the International Reading Association.

From *Read for Your Life* by Joseph Gold, © 1990 Joseph Gold. Reprinted by permission of the author and Fitzhenry & Whiteside Limited.

From *Rock n' Roll and Reading, Part 2: The Next Chapter (1991)*. Reprinted by permission of the Toronto Public Library and CITY-TV/The New Music.

From *The Orphan Boy* by Tololwa Mollel and Paul Morin, text © 1990 Tololwa M. Mollel. Reprinted by permission of Oxford University Press Canada.

From *Wordstruck* by Robert MacNeil, © 1989 Neely Productions Ltd. Reprinted by permission of Viking Penguin USA.

Portions of Chapter 13 have appeared previously in other forms in *The Ottawa Citizen*, *CM* and *Indirections*.

Cover and text design: Tania Craan

Printed and bound in Canada

10 9 8 7 6 5 4 3 2 1

Contents

Acknowledgements

The author would like to thank the many people involved in writing and researching this book: Gale Bildfell, my toughest and best editor; my children and step-children – Jason, Justin, Alex, Ken, and Emma – for at-home and outside research; the various families I taped reading to their children, especially the Bradshaws, Brandons, and Jardines; all the people who wrote or phoned with ideas; Elizabeth Muir, who advised on infant reading, and Myra Johnson, on the reluctant reader; the many parents, teachers, and librarians who looked over chapters and reading lists, including Jane Cobb and Carol McDougall, formerly of the Canadian Children's Book Centre, Pat Hancock, Bryan Prince, Dr. Bob Arnold, Joyce McCorquodale, Chris Rhodes, Janie Jardine, and Pat Deffett; my researcher, Gary Baker, and my chief resource person, Christopher Ball of the OSSTF library. A special nod to Renate Brandon, who kept me writing for a broad audience; Paul Brandon, who ripped up my first drafts, and Shelly Tanaka, my editor, who helped me polish up all the subsequent ones.

Foreword
by Robert Munsch

Just in case you are reading this foreword and wondering whether or not to buy the book: *If you are a parent with kids, you need to read this book.*

Now, on with the foreword. Paul Kropp called me up and asked me to do a foreword to his book on reading. This sounded like the kiss of death to me; I mean, why read a book on reading when I could be really reading a good book instead of reading a book about how my kid isn't reading good books?

Instead of saying no right away, I said I would think about it.

Fatal mistake.

At a writers' meeting in Toronto, up walks Kropp and drops a 300-page typed manuscript into my hands.

"This will help you think," he says.

So I let the pile of unbound pages sit on my desk for two weeks, hoping that it would go into spontaneous combustion, or that Kropp would have a heart attack (hopefully fatal or at least leading to brain death).

After two weeks, my wife happened by.

"Oh, a book on reading. What's it like? Is it any good?"

"Stand there a minute and I will tell you," said I.

I really meant that I would tell her in a minute. I figured that since all books about reading are deadly, it would take me only a minute to verify that for my wife. So I started reading on page six.

I read for a minute and I was on page seven and I said to my wife, "Hey, did you know there is a fourth grade reading slump?"

Recognizing the signs of impending book mania, she said, "Why don't you come and read it at the kitchen table. I hate it when you yell at me from the basement about the book you are reading."

Soon I was at the kitchen table yelling information at my family. By dinner time I was at page 150 and my wife said, "Well, is it any good?"

"Flake off," I said, because I am always rude when people interrupt me when I'm reading a good book. Usually, for me, a good book is science-fiction. Here I was, reading a book on reading and enjoying it.

What's going on? Well, this book is mostly about how family environment and interaction affect children's reading. (It is not about all the abstract reading theory that researchers love to bore you with.) It's about TV, homework, bedtime reading, and why there is a very good chance that your child might stop reading in grade four or grade nine. It is, in short, about the sort of stuff that my wife and I talk and argue about a lot anyway. That is why I ended up reading it at the kitchen table and yelling things out.

Kropp has done a real service by distilling reading theory into meaningful information for families. This sort of book should have been written a long time ago. I hope a lot of parents and a lot of teachers read it.

Introduction

My search for reading solutions began eighteen years ago on the first day I arrived to teach at a vocational high school in Hamilton, Ontario. I hadn't been given this particular teaching assignment because of my years at university studying seventeenth-century poetry, or because I happened to love the works of Shakespeare. I had been sent to Parkview School because I'm over six feet tall and once took wrestling as part of university phys ed.

My assignment was to teach "reading" to teenage boys who either couldn't or wouldn't read much of anything. It meant that I spent two days a week reading a story and answering questions on the blackboard, one day with a noisy filmstrip machine that projected stories line by line on a screen, and two days with a few mouldy novels of the *Moonfleet* variety.

I was struggling through one of those novels with "the guys" – actually young men who ranged in age from thirteen to twenty – when a student I'll call Randy approached me after class. Randy was the smallest person in his group, a slouching boy with large freckles and thick glasses. He always spoke in a whisper.

"Excuse me, sir," he began. "I'm having a little trouble reading the book."

"Oh?"

"Actually, I'm having a lot of trouble," Randy admitted.

"Well, I know it's a bit difficult," I said.

"The truth is, sir, I can't read it at all."

I raised one eyebrow and leaned back in my chair. "Maybe I could give you some extra help after school."

"No, no. That's not what I mean. I mean, *none* of us can read the book, sir."

"None of you?"

"Except Don and Froggy, and they don't really want to read it. The rest of us just can't. The guys asked me to tell you."

"Oh," I said.

"The guys wondered if you could maybe find something else."

"Like what?"

"Like movies, maybe. The teacher before you showed a lot of movies."

It didn't seem to me that movies were the solution to the reading problems of Randy or Froggy or anyone else in that class. What they needed were some books that they *could* read and would *want* to read, books that just didn't exist at the time.

So I set out to write them myself. I began by researching everything I could find about reading, reading difficulty, vocabulary development, and areas of student interest. And I kept checking back with Randy's class.

"It says here," I told them, "that students at your age level are interested in baseball and horses."

The guys looked at each other and shook their heads.

"So what are you interested in?" I asked.

They laughed. "Sex, sir. We're interested in sex!"

When I finally finished my first book, *Burn*

Out, the guys were disappointed that there wasn't much sex. But there was a lot of action, and there were teenage characters they could understand. What's more, I'd taken all my research into reading difficulty and made sure that each page of the book was easy enough for Randy and the others to read on their own.

Since then, besides writing a number of young adult novels for ordinary teenagers, I've written and edited some fifty books for kids who don't much like to read. In the process, the kids themselves have taught me a great deal about reading and writing, and about the kinds of books that work for them.

Back when I was a graduate student, I used to think that reading problems were restricted to a small fraction of the population. I was under the wonderfully naive impression that most children and adults could read well enough to get by. I thought that almost everyone knew the pleasure of sitting down to read a good book.

But I was wrong. What I've learned over the last eighteen years is that literacy is a problem for today's young people. The problem is not limited to students like Randy and Froggy, but extends to many, many kids who aren't reading well – or aren't reading much. Though young children are effectively learning the rudiments of reading in primary school, many of them stop developing as readers in grades four and five. Another group stops bothering to read in grades eight and nine. Among our top students, many have failed to develop the range of sophisticated reading skills they'll need at university and later in life. Worst of all, too many young people today are growing up with attitudes that will always keep them apart from books and the joy that reading can be.

Perhaps that's why you, a parent, feel anxious about your own child's reading. When I travel around the country to talk about my own books, parents keep coming up to ask the same difficult questions:

- "How can I get my child to be a reader?"
- "My son doesn't like to read anything. How can I get him started?"
- "How can I make reading fun?"
- "How can I work with my daughter's teacher to get her reading?"
- "What book would you suggest for my nephew. He's four and . . ."

I finally decided to try to answer all these questions and many others in one book – this one. My hope is that you can use these solutions, from the three Rs in Chapter 1 to the ideas and suggestions in the margins, to help your child become a reader for life.

How to Read This Book

You don't have to read all of this book to get the information you need for your child. I do hope that every parent will tackle the material in the first three chapters because the basic principles are important. After that, you'll likely prefer to go right to the chapter that deals with your child's age group. Chapters 10, 11, and 12 handle special problems – the bored reader, the reluctant reader, and the gifted reader – and will be of particular interest to some parents. The last chapter deals with the larger problems of literacy and government policy in Canada.

Each of the chapters for a particular age group has a number of suggested books listed in the margins and what I've called a "must-have" list at the end of chapter. In creating these lists, I tried to select just a few hundred excellent titles so you can make specific requests of your bookstore or library. I set a goal of having a third of my recommended books by Canadian authors and generally had no problem reaching that number.

The "must-have" lists recommend sixty books worth buying, begging, or borrowing for keeps. These are books of proven appeal, written in many different styles, ranging from picture books to fiction to poetry. Of course, I hope that your child will read many other books as well. In Canada, it's possible for every child to have access to a great variety of books – gifts from relatives, books borrowed from libraries or friends, books on loan from schools or next-door neighbours or picked up for ten cents at a lawn sale. But I feel every child deserves a special bookshelf of truly excellent books to read and reread, perhaps to love. These "must-have" lists contain my choices for that bookshelf.

I have developed these lists based on suggestions from parents, kids, teachers, librarians, and booksellers around the country, yet ultimately the choices are personal. After the titles, I have noted the name of the publisher of the least expensive edition of the book, and the year it was first published. If you find a new title that should be included in the next edition, drop me a note. Better yet, have your son or daughter write the letter, since reading and writing are flip sides of the literacy coin.

The margins also contain other bits and pieces of information – statistics, summaries of research, illustrations from recommended books, addresses and advice that might be helpful to you. In special boxes marked "Parent-to-Parent" I've reprinted suggestions I've received from parents like you. Some of these were in response to a *Globe and Mail* advertisement; some came in during radio phone-in shows; some are from parents I met at conferences – all are valuable ideas based upon the experience of Canadian families.

The goal of all this is to help your child become a reader for life. As a parent, you are essential in making sure that books and the sheer joy of reading are part of your child's experience. No one can encourage reading nearly as well as you can. No other skill you teach or gift you give will ever be quite as important.

CHAPTER 1

Why *You* Are Essential

If you stop to consider what's involved in learning to read, it should come as no surprise that your child will need your help to become a reader for life.

Between the ages of four and nine, your child will have to master some 100 phonics rules, learn to recognize 3,000 words with just a glance, and develop a comfortable reading speed approaching 100 words a minute. He must learn to combine words on the page with a half-dozen squiggles called punctuation into something – a voice or image in his mind – that gives back meaning.

And that's just the beginning. Between the ages of nine and fifteen, your child will have to double that reading speed, expand his recognition vocabulary to 100,000 words, learn to skim over some sections of print and to slow down to study others, all while he simultaneously questions the text and appreciates the author's artistry. The novelist John Steinbeck summed up the task of learning to read as "the greatest single effort that the human mind undertakes, and he must do it as a child."

But your child cannot do it alone. To become a

1

real reader, your child needs you. Your child needs a parent who will

- read to him;

- listen to his reading when he's young;

- talk to him about his reading when he's older;

- organize a quiet time so reading can happen;

- buy or borrow books and other reading material;

- work with his teachers at school;

- serve as a model of adult reading and interest in books.

Without you, your child is unlikely to develop the attitudes that make reading easy and fun. Without you, your child can fall into that fourth grade reading slump that affects a third of our children. Without you, your child may well lose interest in reading at age twelve or thirteen, just when he's capable of crossing over to adult books. Without you, your child is unlikely to become a reader for life.

Unfortunately, learning to read is not an easy task. It isn't like learning to walk, for instance, because the specific instinct for reading isn't part of our genetic make-up. Nor is learning to read like learning to bat a ball or play the piano. If our children show little talent for baseball or music, we know that life offers many other outlets for their energy and creativity. But if our children don't learn to read, they are virtually crippled as they attempt to deal with modern life.

At one time, of course, the skill of reading was required by only a limited portion of the population. Medieval kings and queens had letters and manuscipts read to them. Medieval peasants lived in a world of spoken language and had little reason to read themselves. Right up until the nineteenth century, fewer than one person in ten – even in Western countries – was able to read. When Charles Dickens' great novels first appeared in the 1830s, they weren't snapped up by masses of Englishmen and women eager for the latest best-seller. They were bought in instalments, like magazines, by families and groups of friends who might have only one "reader" among them. It was the job of the reader to read the book out loud to the rest of the family, or to the mates at work, or at the pub.

Throughout most of history, reading has been done out loud. Renaissance accounts of the Bodleian Library at Oxford University comment on the noise made by dozens of scholars all reading out loud at once. The very first 'Shhh!' in libraries wasn't to stop people from talking; it was to stop scholars from reading too loudly for their neighbours.

Silent, private reading was an invention of the Victorian age. For most of human history, reading had been a public activity. Novels were read to family groups gathered around the hearth; poetry was performed with musical accompaniment after a feast; married couples read to each other before going to bed. Reading, because it took place out loud, was a social event.

It still should be. Most families today know that reading books out loud is very important for young children. According to a 1991 study done for Canada's Department of Communications, almost two-thirds of all families with children under the age of fourteen say they regularly find time to read aloud. These families are reported to spend an average of twenty-two minutes a day reading, or listening to their children read, or talking about what's read.

Sadly, the same study reveals that family time spent reading together declines rapidly as children get older. Apparently, only a tiny fraction of families read out loud together for more than a few years in their child's life. Parents are too busy. Or they're too tired. Or it's easier to turn on

Furore for Dickens

Long before the works of Charles Dickens were mummified in school curricula, they were raging popular successes. Most were published first in serial form — a chapter or so each month — like a magazine. When *The Old Curiosity Shop* (1841) reached its final instalment, readers around the world were desperate to know the end. In New York City, 6,000 people gathered on the wharf awaiting the ship that carried the final chapter, some even calling out to the sailors, "Does Little Nell die?"

Do You Read with Your Child?

When the results of the Reading in Canada 1991 study came out, I was pleased to tell a conference of booksellers that 62 percent of parents surveyed said they regularly read with their children.

Educator David Booth quickly replied, "That's absurd. Any teacher could tell you that only one child in five has parents who read to him."

So what's the true figure? The Department of Communications survey began when 23,900 people were asked if they would complete a written survey. Only half agreed. Of the 12,000 surveys mailed out, only 7,000 came back completed, probably by fairly literate individuals. What about the 17,000 people who didn't want to be part of the study? Do they read to their children?

the television or pop in a video. And the kid can read for himself, anyway, can't he? And what are schools for if they don't make the kids read? And . . . and . . . There are so many excuses – as many excuses as there are teenagers who can't be bothered to read.

This is a terrible shame. There are many joys for both parents and children in reading out loud that I see no reason to call it quits just because a child has mastered enough of the basics to begin reading himself.

How long should you and your child keep reading together? Frankly, I don't think families should ever stop reading together. The educated elite have always read aloud to each other and used reading as a focal point for discussion and imagination. Only in our time have we turned reading into a solitary activity.

Reading out loud isn't nearly as difficult or time-consuming as it might seem. A short story can be read aloud in about thirty minutes. A magazine or newspaper article frequently takes less time. Even an adult novel, read twenty minutes a day, can often be finished in two or three weeks.

Many books are now available on tape, read by their authors or by professional actors with wonderful verve and flair. I know a single father who drives with his children from Toronto to a cottage in Haliburton every other Friday night in the summer months. The trip takes about three hours – just enough time to listen to a tape of Charles Dicken's *David Copperfield* or Anne Rice's *Interview with a Vampire* or Sue Grafton's *G is for Gumshoe* which he borrows from the public library. It is almost the same as reading used to be a century ago, except that the tape deck has become the "reader." And just as at any social reading throughout history, the "reader" will be asked to repeat sections (the rewind button), or to stop (pause button) while the family asks questions about the plot or shares an idea that the story has prompted.

If we think of reading as sharing, we can see how important the social aspect must be. Reading lets us access our collective experience, to harvest the skills and wisdom of all humanity. And reading brings joy – the sheer fun of stepping into other lives, other universes – of getting caught up in a world of imagination.

It is for these reasons that all of us want our children to be readers for life.

The Basics

Your child will not become a reader for life overnight, or in sixty days, or because I can offer you a handful of gimmicks to make it happen. Your child will become a reader with your loving involvement and your commitment to a process that stretches from infancy to the teenage years and beyond. Here are three basic rules to get you started:

The Basics: The Three Rs

1. Read with your child every day.

2. Reach into your wallet to buy books, magazines, and other reading material for your child and yourself.

3. Rule the TV. Put a reasonable limit on television, video, and video games so there will be time for reading in your child's life.

---

1. Read with your child every day.
You and your child deserve a regular reading time, fifteen to thirty minutes long, every day. Don't begin with a plan to read every other day, or twice a week, or whenever you happen to feel like it. You are going to miss days even with the

best of intentions. Your commitment should be for every day so that the books you read will have some continuity. You know that if you put a novel down for a week, you'll likely have a hard time picking up the threads of the story. It is just as difficult for your child. Reading time should become a habit for you, something that is expected by your child, an activity you can both anticipate with pleasure.

Where you read doesn't matter – in your child's bedroom, on a reading chair, in the living room. When you read doesn't matter – after school, after dinner, before bed. How well you read doesn't matter. All of us, as parents, are the best readers for our own children.

What does matter is that you read *with* your child, not just *to* your child. Reading time is not simply time to open a book and read out loud. It's time to open a book to share reading and ideas. As parents, I think we do this almost instinctively. When I tape-recorded mothers and fathers reading aloud for this book, many apologized to me for talking to their children so much during their daily reading time. It was as if they had done something wrong instead of doing exactly what oral reading is all about.

"Words make another place, a place to escape to with your spirit alone. Every child entranced by reading stumbles on that blissful experience sooner or later."
– Robert MacNeil, *Wordstruck*

Since reading is a social experience, it should always be accompanied by cuddling, talking, joking, and asking and answering questions. Especially for older children, some of the most valuable reading experiences are *not* reading; they come with the talk that is prompted by the book.

Many families go through a period of stress that can seriously affect their children. Divorce, unemployment, family tension – all can interfere with a child's development. In such situations, family reading time can be a single, still point in the centre of an emotional storm. Adults whose own childhoods were in turmoil often look back on such quiet moments, time spent together with a loving parent, as essential for getting through a difficult period. And the benefits of a quiet half hour spent reading together are not just for your child.

At some point, your child will naturally want to take over some of the reading from you. This doesn't mean that your reading out loud should stop; it means that your efforts have been a success and should continue.

The first reading most children do comes from memory. You'll have read one book so often that your child knows the book by heart. Your child will then want to "read" it to you, because your nightly reading will have shown just how important reading is. Later, as your child learns to recognize more words and perhaps sound out a word or two, the memorized text will be more read than remembered. And later still, on nights when Mom is too tired or Dad wants to quit before the end of the chapter, your child will want to read on – out loud – to you.

Just be careful you don't respond to this success by getting lax about the daily reading. There are many important reasons for you to keep reading out loud with your child as long as you possibly can.

When your child enters grade one, he can understand roughly 6,000 spoken words but can read only 100 or so. Both of these numbers continue to grow through elementary school, until, some time around grade eight, your child's listening and reading vocabularies will become equal. All through elementary school, your child needs your help to understand the meanings of new, more difficult words, sentences, and ideas. He needs a parent to look up what a mandible is or explain why there's no triceratops at the zoo. He needs you to laugh with him at a Gordon Korman novel as much as he needed you to help sound out the handful of words in P.D. Eastman's *Are You My Mother?* As a parent, you should keep reading – or at least being there for the reading and the talk – as long as your child will let you. Why would you cut short such a delightful family time any sooner?

Parent-to-Parent
Comics Are Books, Too

"There were no books in my house when we were growing up, so I suppose it's surprising that I grew up to love reading. What was important for me was my father's example – he was always taking night school courses to improve his English.

"And then there were comic books. At the time, my family couldn't afford to buy real books and my school library consisted of a book cart pushed from room to room. But comic books even I could afford – they were only a quarter – and I was able to read them over and over again."

– Robert Sisti, Newmarket, Ontario

Sometimes, family reading can yield results that are quite astounding. I knew a family in Hamilton who read regularly with all four of their children. The first three children were very bright. They quickly became readers themselves, and went on to university and professional careers. The family's last child – I'll call her Dana – was diagnosed as developmentally handicapped at birth and spent much of her life in special schools and special classes. Nonetheless, the family kept reading with Dana, knowing that books would enrich her life. Dana's mother says, "We treated her just like the other children, even though the doctors told us that our daughter was limited and we couldn't expect very much from her."

I taught Dana in a regular grade ten class in which we were studying *Of Mice and Men* by John Steinbeck. After reading the first chapter of the novel out loud, I asked the kids to continue on their own since my throat was sore. There were the usual grumbles of protest, but it was Dana who raised her hand. "I'll read chapter two, sir." And she did, with fluency and distinctive voices and wonderful animation, all with no help from me.

After four years, Dana went out on a co-op program to work at a library where her bright smile and fluent reading brought delight to everyone. Today, she still works as a library helper and still loves to read. Dana has done far better, in fact, than many of her "normal" classmates. And her achievements, I think, are a tribute both to her and to her family, and to the fact that they never stopped reading out loud together.

2. Reach into your wallet to buy books, magazines, and other reading material for your child and yourself.

Your child should have his own books on a special bookshelf someplace in the home. Books from the library and school are wonderful, and books borrowed from friends are important, but nothing can replace books of one's own.

Why? Because the books your child owns are the ones that you'll read to him over and over again. And the books that are read to your child over and over again at ages two and three become the first books your child will read for himself at ages four and five. These are the books he will keep going back to, reading and rereading, sometimes long after you would think they'd been outgrown. One study says that some of the books on your child's bookshelf will be read as many as 300 times before he begins to lose interest in them. This kind of repeated rereading is important for building reading skills, but it can happen only when your child has his own books.

I wish every family in Canada could afford to buy a book a month for their children. Children need a wide range of books in order to find the ones they'll read over and over again. When our first child was two, my wife and I wanted Jason to enjoy a picture book of E.B. White's *Charlotte's Web* or one of the other gorgeous books he'd received from his grandparents. But the book Jason really loved was an inexpensive, easy-to-read book called *Hand, Hand, Fingers, Thumb* by Al Perkins. E.B. White's classic was a wonderful read for my wife and me, but *Hand, Hand, Fingers, Thumb* had rhythm, rhyme and action written into the story. I ended up reading the book to Jason so many times that today, twenty years later, I can still recite most of the book from memory. It's no wonder that *Hand, Hand, Fingers, Thumb* became the first book Jason "read" for himself at age four.

The point I'm making is that it is very hard for us, as parents, to guess which books will be our child's favourites. I can suggest, as I do later on, that Louise Fitzhugh's *Harriet the Spy* or Jean Little's *Mama's Gonna Buy You a Mockingbird* might well become a favourite. But only your child can make that choice.

If you try to add a book a month to your child's bookshelf, each new book will be another chance to find one that might become a favourite. If not,

Parent-to-Parent
Egg and a Book

"I've raised three children and all three are now readers. I suppose they always saw their father and me with our noses in a book, but we made sure we did more than that. Books were always part of our children's lives. At Christmas and birthdays, whatever the other presents, there was always a book. Even at Easter, when other kids might get piles of chocolates in the Easter baskets, my kids got chocolates, an Easter egg, and a book."

– Elizabeth Crangle,
  Peterborough, Ontario

Reading Makes Attitude

Dr. Alan King of Queen's University surveyed 46,000 Ontario high school students between 1983 and 1985. He found –

"The over 9,000 respondents who said they read only one hour or less a week . . . are more likely to

- have low self-esteem;
- have a less satisfying relationship with parents;
- have a negative attitude towards school; and
- be experiencing difficulty in school."

at least you and your child have had an opportunity to read something new together.

Buying books for your child need not be terribly expensive. Libraries frequently offer books no longer in circulation for less than a dollar each. Second-hand bookstores sometimes have an excellent range of children's books from fifty cents for a paperback novel to five dollars for a gorgeous picture book. Lawn sales are good sources for cast-off books with prices that may start off at a dollar a title in the morning, but often come down to pennies by the end of the day.

For young families, grandparents and other relatives are a wonderful source of books. When I was a graduate student living on a few thousand dollars a year, we couldn't afford to buy beautiful picture books for our sons. But my parents could, and Aunt Carol could, and sometimes friends would pass on a book that their kids no longer read. If you put the word out that you'd like to receive books for your child, then birthdays and Christmas and Hanukkah will bring many new titles for your child's bookshelf.

Still, the most exciting way to acquire books is a trip to the bookstore. It gives your child a chance to choose his own brand-spanking-new books with that wonderful feel only new books have. Your child will pick books just as you and I do – just as any reader does – by the cover, or by the backcover blurb, or by what his friends recommend. Yet real-life choices always have to be tempered by real-life limitations. It's your money that's being spent, even if it's only on a tiny ninety-nine-cent Annikin or a remaindered picture book on sale for $2.99. It's quite fair for you not to fork out for another Sweet Valley High novel, or to suggest that *Up to Low* by Brian Doyle really is a better book than whatever Saturday-morning-cartoon spin-off might be on display. Because reading is a social experience, both you and your child should have a say in what's purchased and what's read. Just remember that the act of choosing a book, like the act of reading, is empowering for your child. Try to support that choice as much as you reasonably can.

One family I know always buys two books for their ten-year-old son when they go to the bookstore. One is chosen entirely by the child, another is chosen together with the parents. The family sets a price limit on each book that might be lower than what they could spend on just one title, but the method gives an important message. It's vitally important that you listen to your child and try to respect the books he loves; but it's just as important that you enjoy what you buy and read together. There are some 30,000 children's books in print and another 4,500 appearing every year. Don't lose the joy of reading by spending too such time or money on books that give you, the parent, no pleasure. There are many more that will bring delight to both you and your child.

And while you're at the bookstore, why not buy a book or two for yourself? You're not just a parent, you're a model. If you read, your child is likely to read. If you surround yourself with books and magazines, so will your child. According to research, most readers come from families with a wide assortment of books, magazines, and newspapers around the house. You don't have to be rich to make your home "print rich." This kind of rich is an attitude towards books – an attitude that says books are worth reading.

Some years ago, I taught at a school that encouraged teachers to visit the families of students. I remember going into a dismal apartment building where the single father of my best student lived. The father's apartment wasn't in much better condition than the building, with yellowed paint and cracked linoleum floors. But John's father had made the place "print rich," with books, newspapers, pamphlets, catalogues, church flyers, coffee-table books, car-repair manuals – more print than I had at my house. And John was a reader.

I also visited the home of a teenage boy whose

Such a Pity

When Benjamin Franklin, the famous inventor and publisher, was serving as American ambassador to France, he often impressed French intellectuals with the wisdom of his remarks. At one dinner, the question was raised, "What human condition deserves the most pity?" Each of the guests responded, but the answer that is still remembered is Benjamin Franklin's: "A lonesome man on a rainy day who does not know how to read."

reading skills never got beyond *Scuffy the Tugboat.* Ron's parents kept a tidy home and were at a loss to understand why their son didn't read. "We have books," they said, pointing to a single shelf of encyclopaedias, Reader's Digest condensed books and a half-dozen yellowed paperbacks. There was no other printed material in the house. When asked, Ron's parents told me they never read magazines or newspapers. I guessed from their bookshelf that they didn't read books, either. Yet the mother was convinced Ron's illiteracy was caused by some brain damage no doctor could detect.

The point is this: you'll never make your child a reader for life by telling him that reading is important. You have to show him. Even if you're not a reader or you've fallen out of the habit of reading, you'll find pleasure in reading with your child. Let that be a basis for making your home "print rich" – buying some books, borrowing many others, and reading with your child every day.

High School: Books and TV

- Average number of hours an Ontario high school student says he or she spends reading each week: 5.8
- Number of hours watching TV: 13.6
- Number of hours playing video games: 2.0

3. **Rule the TV. Put a reasonable limit on television, video, and video games so there will be time for reading in your child's life.**

By grade eight, the average Canadian child will have spent 12,000 hours in front of the television set. He will have seen 300,000 commercials and more than 10,000 murders on the small screen. He will have watched everything from cartoons to R-rated and sometimes X-rated movies. He will have spent more hours watching televison than he has in school – more hours being a passive observer than he will spend on anything else in his life except sleeping.

Too many hours.

There is a growing body of research to indicate that if your child watches more than three hours of television a day he will suffer problems in reading, at school, and in social development.

A recent study by Caroline Snow of Harvard University reinforces this. Dr. Snow writes about the importance of family in the reading achievement of children. She demonstrated again what researchers have long known – that families who have books around the house tend to have children who read. She also found that the educational expectations set by the mother are very important in motivating a child to be a reader.

But Dr. Snow's most striking finding was about television. Her study determined that the most important factor affecting reading that is under the direct control of a parent is "rules on watching television." Students from families who set rules on television watching made signficantly greater progress in developing both reading and general literacy than families without rules.

Dr. Alan King of Queen's University in Kingston came up with similar results when he looked at adolescents in Ontario. Where television watching was reported to be high, school success was frequently low.

In the Ontario high school system, students are streamed into three levels – basic, general, and advanced. Basic-level students take courses leading to jobs like auto body work and building construction. Advanced students are in programs aimed at university or community college.

Dr. King found that the proportion of basic-level students watching television more than thirty hours a week was twice as high as that of advanced-level students. The proportion of basic-level students who played video games more than ten hours a week was three times higher than that of advanced level students. Significantly, nearly one-quarter of basic-level students in the study said they did not read at all.

The research is clear – too much television can interfere with the intellectual development of children. Unfortunately, the research can't tell you exactly how much TV is too much. Nor can it tell you exactly what rules to apply to the television viewing of your child, in your family, where you live.

Nonetheless, I would suggest that three hours

How Much TV Is Too Much?

Many studies show that reading time declines as TV watching goes up – and some show declining reading skills as a result. But pinpointing just how much TV is too much becomes harder. According to Susan Neuman of the University of Lowell in Massachusetts, there is little statistical difference in children's reading skills whether they watch two or three hours of TV a day. But beyond four hours a day, "the effects were negative and increasingly deleterious."

David Suzuki's Solution: A VCR

David Suzuki has a solution to the violence and commercialism on television. In his family, all shows are videotaped first; then Suzuki quickly previews the programs before the kids see them.

Not only does this give parents some control over what children see on the screen, it gives everyone a chance to fast-forward over the commercials.

of television a day is probably more than enough for any child. The virtue of the "three-hours-a-day maximum" rule is its simplicity. Research is unclear on the effect of less TV watching; it is very clear that more than three hours a day is not good for your children.

Of course, you'll have to talk to your children about how that three hours a day will be applied. May they watch no TV one day and six hours the next? Does a PBS special count? Are videos part of the total? The rules you set should work for you, your partner, and your children. Like any parental rules, they should be firm without being etched in stone. But there must be rules. Your child *will not* become a better student after another hour of Nintendo, or *Gilligan's Island,* or the latest blood-and-gore video. Your child *will* do better in school if there's some quiet time at home – to read, to write a story, to dream.

One of the most wonderful suggestions I received for this book came from Regis O'Conner, a teacher in Sault Ste Marie, Ontario. In raising his four children, he set aside the hour after supper, from seven to eight o'clock, as a quiet time. "The TV went off, there was no music, no radio, no stereo, no distractions. The rules were the same for us and for the kids. We could do one of three things – read, draw, or do homework. When the hour was up, the TV could go back on, or the kids could play a record or do whatever they wanted, but frequently we would keep on reading, or drawing or just thinking." The O'Conner family members are scattered now all over the province but all the children became avid readers.

Setting rules on television – creating a time for reading to happen – will not be easy. Your young children will feel no hesitation in telling you about Billy next door who watches cartoons with breakfast and *Saturday Night Live* while he's going to sleep. Your older children may offer very compelling arguments about the intellectual importance of *The Simpsons* and the reputed excellence of tonight's made-for-TV docudrama. You'll be told that "all the kids" have a Nintendo or some such device, and that your children will be social outcasts if they don't have one, too. In fact, there is a tremendous industry – from television into movies and toys – that profits at the expense of your child's real development.

You have to stand up in the midst of all that and say no. No, the TV won't be on after 9:30 PM. No, one hour of a video game is enough. No, there is more to life than another Arnold Schwarzenegger movie.

By doing that, you'll make sure there's time for reading in your child's life. If you make sure there are books available to fill that time, and you offer your own involvement to help read those books, you can virtually ensure that your child will become a reader for life.

How Well Does a Person Have to Read?

The readability of a piece of writing is sometimes measured by the years of schooling required for the average person to understand it.

Print source	Years of school necessary
Toronto *Sun* news reports	6 to 8 years
The Handmaid's Tale, a novel by Margaret Atwood	8.5 to 10 years
Toronto *Sun*, sports	8 to 12 years
Globe and Mail, editorial	10 years
Globe and Mail, news	12 years
Federal Family Allowance inserts	10 to 12 years
How to Apply for Your Social Insurance Number	13 to 17+ years
Ontario Workers Compensation Board guide	16 to 17+ years

CHAPTER 2

Learning to Read – Throughout Life

One of the most wonderful aspects of being a parent is being part of the process by which your child becomes a reader. In modern life, reading has become so tied into children's growth that each stage in learning to read offers a window on that stage of childhood.

When your infant holds up a storybook and begins to babble as if she were reading, she's experimenting with talking and the idea of a book. When your child begins decoding those first few words in a favourite book, she's trying to gain mastery over print and the whole world of language. Later, as your child gains confidence and fluency in reading, her bookshelf will mirror her exploration of the world outside your home. Then, in her teenage years, your child will offer critical commentary on everything from J.R.R. Tolkien to her history textbook, just as she often looks critically at herself, at you, and at the world she's moving into.

Obviously, learning to read doesn't happen at just a single time in your child's life. Learning to read is a process, developed in stages, and your role as a parent is somewhat different at each stage.

In this chapter, I'd like to set some ground-work by explaining why almost every child wants to learn how to read. Then I'll look at the usual stages in reading development, so you can understand how reading grows and changes for your child. I'll describe briefly how reading is taught in school and how you can support it. Then I'll focus on the two danger times for young readers – grade four and grade nine – so you can be aware of steps you can take to keep your child reading right to adulthood.

Motivation: Why Your Child Wants To Read

Given the chance, almost every child wants to learn to read. You can see the desire in infants studying picture books, in second graders carefully sounding out difficult words, in the fact that more than ninety percent of our children have mastered the basics of reading by the end of grade three. For so many children to read so well, so early, the motivation must be strong.

If you understand why your child wants to be a reader, you can help her along the way. And you can avoid some of the pitfalls and gimmicks on the market that won't help your child in the long run.

Here are five reasons why your child wants to learn to read:

- Reading helps a child make sense of the world she lives in.

- Reading is a vital social skill for everything from school to video games.

- Reading is fun.

- Reading is a wonderful way to spend time together with you.

- Reading must be a very grown-up activity, because Mom and Dad are always doing it.

From your child's perspective, the world is a pretty confusing place. In the first few years of life, she must try to make sense of the end product of several thousand years of civilization – everything from the proper use of a spoon to how to program the VCR. There is no better tool to help in this task than reading. My own children learned every city between Oshawa and Hamilton by reading the maps on the train long before they officially knew phonics or could even read a whole sentence. Once your child understands that the word *Oakville* means "We'd better get ready to get off the train," she'll understand that reading gives us control over our lives.

Your child will also see that reading is a vital social skill. There is enormous peer pressure to read all the signs and symbols of modern life. One of the big motivating factors in my own reading development was the game of Monopoly. My older sister and her friends made it clear that I wasn't going to be able to play Monopoly with them until I could read the property deeds myself. No wonder my early reading vocabulary was full of words like *Pacific* and *Boardwalk*.

Reading is also great fun. Your child will find delight in the challenge of sounding out a tough word, or reading a difficult story aloud, just as you might enjoy tackling a crossword puzzle. Success at early reading tasks will bolster your child's sense of self-esteem, as well as give her mastery over the world around her.

Finally, I can't emphasize enough your own importance as a motivator for reading. Your attitude towards reading – expressed in what you do more than in what you say – is vital in motivating your child to be a reader. If you take the time to read with your child every day, then the physical act of reading will always be associated in her mind with warmth, safety and love. If you surround yourself with books, magazines, and newspapers, and make time to read yourself, then your child will see reading as something adults do. According to statistics, your attitude towards reading is the strongest predictor of

The Harvard Study

Caroline Snow and her associates at Harvard University did a long-term study on home factors affecting literacy. Here are the factors that encourage childhood reading, ranked in order of their effect:

- **1.** home "literacy" environment: books, newspapers, attitudes;
- **2.** mother's educational expectations of the child;
- **3.** mother's own education;
- **4.** parent-child interaction.

The father's expectations and background apparently had no effect on reading, but they were important in promoting the child's writing development.

Parent-to-Parent
Making Books

"My mother and I made books even before I knew how to read. These would be pictures-only books, carefully drawn and coloured by me, then sewn together with my mother. Eventually I got the pictures to tell a story. Then reading just seemed to follow naturally."
– Wenda Watt, Toronto, Ontario

whether or not your child will be a reader. That's why you are so important all along the way.

Because the forces that motivate reading are so strong and so important in a child's life, parents shouldn't have to add artificial incentives or gimmicks. No child will learn to read because you tell her that someday she'll be able to appreciate Shakespeare. No child will be motivated for long by the promise of a gold star in her workbook or an A on a report card. No child will be much interested in reading books that have nothing to do with her own life, even if you pay her a quarter a title to do so. All these rewards – these gimmicks – are external to the reading. They don't connect with the social aspects of reading or with children's basic curiosity about books and life. The real motivation for reading must always be found in reading itself – and the books, magazines, and stories that go with that. You can encourage this best by being part of your child's reading and by modelling reading for her. These acts are what create readers for life.

Stage One: The Idea of Reading

The first stage in learning to read is to understand that there is meaning in the words and pictures on a page. This stage frequently begins in infancy, even before your child's first birthday. She'll have sat on your lap and heard you talk through so many picture books that she understands the *idea* of a book even before she can even say the word. When your child sees a stop sign, you'll read the word *stop* and then explain what it means and why you have to do it. The explanation may not make much sense to your two-year-old, but the connection between a printed word (and the red octagonal sign) and an action (stopping the car) demonstrates that words are out there for a reason. Your child begins learning very early that words and books bring meaning to a complex world.

Stage Two: Cracking the Code

When your child begins reading by herself, her progress will be made in fits and starts. There will be a word or two, a sentence or two, lots of mistakes and gradual correction. Your child won't begin reading with the rules of phonics; she'll begin with words: *stop, Mom, Daddy, Teenage Mutant Ninja Turtles.* Our printed language is a code. Once your child understands that it's possible to decode these strange marks on the page, she'll naturally want to try to read them.

New Zealand educator Sylvia Ashton Warner used children's curiosity about their own world to help Maori children begin reading. She wrote out lists of words that pertained to her students' lives, from *mumps* to *helicopter,* words that worked far better than any purchased flashcards. You can use the same method to write out lists of words that pertain to your child's life — *Auntie Sylvia, Ralph the dog, Nintendo.* Or you could write *milk* on the milk container, or stick some magnetic letters on the fridge, starting with your child's name. As a parent, you can make words and reading fun for preschoolers.

The only serious mistakes you could make are to turn reading into work or to expect too much from your child. There are any number of preschool phonics programs on the market. Sometimes, for some children, they actually work. But I wonder what the hurry is. Your child is going to learn to read – at her own pace, in her own way – without having to listen to an audio tape on phonic blending just before bedtime. Far better to associate reading with books, discovery, fun, and your love than to turn it into a childhood task done to earn parental approval.

If you read regularly with your child, the movement from simple word recognition to more complex reading will happen quite naturally. Sometimes it occurs so swiftly as to seem almost miraculous. One day your child seems to be struggling along, reading a word here, a word

One-third of 500,000 = 22?

There are almost half a million words in our English language – the largest language on earth, incidentally – but a third of all our writing is made up of only twenty-two words. Here they are:

a, of, and, that, he, the, I, to, in, was, it, all, had, said, as, have, so, at, him, they, be, his, we, but, not, with, are, on, you, for, one.

Father May Know Best

According to Peter Brennan of the North York Board of Education, fathers are better at helping their children to read because they're less patient than mothers. When a child comes across an unfamiliar word, mothers tend to make the child sound it out. Dad is more likely to tell the child the word or tell him to skip it and carry on. Dad's approach keeps the story moving.

there. Two or three weeks later, she's zipping through a familiar book, reading to you with obvious joy and pride.

We will likely never understand all the factors that make this first reading breakthrough happen, nor can we be sure just how it will take place for your child. For some children, reading simply clicks. Suddenly, the child can recognize many words, and seems to have created some internal rules for how our language works. What's more, the recognition of words and sentences becomes generalized so the *hop* in *Hop on Pop* can appear in any book, or a number of different type faces, and still be recognized. Often this all happens at home, well before your child attends school.

For other children, the progress is less dramatic. Gradually, more words are recognized, reading speed slowly increases, longer words are sounded out or guessed at successfully. It probably makes little long-term difference whether your child's reading seems to click or develops more slowly. There is no real evidence a child who makes a breakthrough into reading at age three or four ultimately reads any better than a child who progresses more slowly from age four to seven. Far more important is your support of your child's reading, however and whenever she begins.

Stage Three: Learning at School

Chances are that when your child enters kindergarten she will already read far more than children did thirty years ago. She can probably identify a very personal assortment of words, or read a few favourite books, or sound out and blend together some of the words she's seen on *Sesame Street*. The job of your child's school is to take these beginning skills and develop them so she can read much more widely.

How your child's school tackles this challenge

depends on the teacher, the books used, and the approach that underlies the teaching.

When I grew up in the 1950s, the primers given to children were heavily based on phonics. Phonics is a system for decoding words based on what their phonic bits sound like (*sn*. . ."sna". . . long *a* . . ."ay". . . *k* . . ."kuh". . . silent *e* makes the *a* long) and how they blend together ("snake"). Phonics works quite well in languages like German where words almost invariably "sound-out" quite easily. In English, unfortunately, only about sixty-five percent of our words can be easily decoded using the phonics approach. The others are exceptions, or need additional information from context. Nor is phonics a particularly easy system. One series of readers presents 240 phonics bits for young children to master. Other series have offered as many as 120 different rules for blending the phonic bits together. Even though phonics is helpful in tackling unfamiliar words – and, later on, for spelling – the whole system can be enough to boggle any young mind.

The big competing technique used to be "look-say," or "whole word recognition." In this approach, children are helped to identify many hundreds of words without any formal training in phonics. From this, most children develop rules in their own minds which help them attack unfamiliar words. While students schooled in phonics seem to do better in reading unfamiliar words out loud, students taught by the look-say method seem to do better understanding the meaning behind what they read.

The most popular approach these days is neither phonics nor look-say, but "whole language." The whole language approach to reading places its focus on stories and the child's response to them. "Whole language" means that reading, writing, and thinking are all integrated into lessons based on a piece of children's literature. A skilled teacher can do a unit on outer space and

Phonic Bits

Learning to read with phonics requires the student to master the sound of a number of phonic bits. Here's a sampling:

- Consonants: initial consonants like the *b* in *blend*; final consonants like the *r* in *computer*.
- Vowels: long vowels like the *i* in *like*; short vowels like the *o* in *short*.
- Digraphs: special two-letter combinations like *ch, wh, ck, ng, qu, wr*.
- Blends: letter combinations that must be blended together like *pl, fr, str, nk, br*.
- Diphthongs: vowel combinations like *ay, ea, oo, oi, ay*.
- Phonograms: special combinations like *ide, ame, ook, ight, tion*.

School Reading Programs Over 100 Years

The idea of an organized reading series has seen many changes. Here are some samples:

From *McGuffey's First Eclectic Reader* (1890)

Lesson XXXIV:

See my dear, old grandma in her easy-chair! How gray her hair is! She wears glasses when she reads.

She is always kind, and takes such good care of me that I like to do what she tells me.

From *Fun With Dick and Jane* (W.J. Gage & Co., 1940)

FATHER HELPS THE FAMILY

Mother said, "Oh, Father! Will you do something for me? Will you please help me?"

"I will see," said Father. "I will see."

Jane said, "Look, Father. Will you please help me? You work for Mother. Can you work for me, too?"

"I will see," said Father.

have a whole class reading words like *Jupiter* and *mission control* long before the old phonics-based primers would even reach the J words. When done well, the whole language approach can be wonderfully exciting; when done poorly, it at least doesn't do much damage. By and large, the whole language approach, mixed with some phonics exercises, is enough to help your child master the reading skills she needs up to a grade three level.

In the past, some schools were guilty of quite disasterous experiments in the teaching of reading. In the 1950s some Commonwealth schools got hooked on a system called Initial Teaching Alphabet, in which all the early stories were written in a special forty-four-letter phonetic alphabet. The system worked fine until the kids had to read real English. In the early 1960s, Chicago schools virtually banned phonics from their schools – until standardized reading tests showed a terrible drop in skills. But, as far as I know, no Canadian school is doing anything quite so radical these days. For at least the first three grades, you can probably rely on your child's school to give her the formal reading instruction she needs to get started.

Stage Four: Growing Competence

By the end of grade three, and often long before, your child will have mastered enough of the basics to handle many different kinds of reading material. The act of decoding the page will come so quickly and so easily that some parents might feel the process of learning to read is complete.

Don't be fooled by early success. Reading is not just decoding words on a page. It is not just reading a passage and answering the questions. It is not just a trick your child has to do to get from grade three to grade four.

Reading is dreaming. Reading is entering a world of imagination shared between reader and author. Reading is getting beyond the words to the story or the meaning underneath.

Read with me the opening of Tololwa Mollel's *The Orphan Boy*:

> As he had done every night of his life, the old man gazed deep into the heavens. He had spent so such time scanning the night sky that he knew every star it held. He loved the stars as if they were his children. He always felt less lonely when the sky was clear and the stars formed a glowing canopy over the plains.
>
> Tonight, he noticed, one of the stars was missing.

Even without Paul Morin's illustrations, the text of this wonderful children's book transports us from where we are – this author at the word processor, you in your chair – to the night world outside. We move from life within ourselves, from the simple workmanlike prose of this non-fiction book, to words that have a special magic. The night sky *holds* its stars in a *glowing canopy*. The old man, who must often feel lonely just as we all do, feels reassured by the stars. Until one is missing – and with his, our hearts skip a beat.

Reading the words is really only a tool for entering into the dreams, ideas, and feelings behind them. Just as when playing the piano, the student must get beyond the keys and notes to play the music, so when reading a book, your child must get beyond the code to reach the author's images or concepts, or experience.

By middle school, your child will have mastered enough of the mechanics of reading – vocabulary, quick sounding out, fluent reading speed – that these are no longer the prime concern. The task now, both in school and at home, is to broaden and deepen the reading. The trick is to do this while keeping the excitement of books and the joy of reading.

Your child now will have enough mastery of reading to use books for her own ends. She'll use

From *Impressions*, "Writing Resource Centre" (Holt, Rinehart and Winston, 1984), Grade 1.

One day a princess
was going to town.
She got lost.
A swan found her.
The swan was nice.
She flew home on the back of
the swan.
The swan changed into a prince.
The prince and the princess
became friends.
And then _____

(student completes story)

Resources: The Public Library

We have over 1,700 public libraries in Canada, ranging from storefront operations to million-book reference collections. Any public library will have thousands of books for your child – and much more . . .

- Story hours. Little kids love to be read to, and librarians are trained to do it well.

- Films, author visits, and other events. Your public library is also a community centre.

- Video and audio tapes. The video collection frequently has classics you won't find at the milk store. Books on tapes come with the books for kids; separately for adults.

- Fun and games. Many libraries now check out games ranging from Scrabble to Lego.

- Literacy programs. Some public libraries offer reading programs for adults with weak reading skills. If not, they'll know where to send you.

- On-line computers. Doing research? Some library research services are tied into the *Globe and Mail*'s Infonet.

- Advice. In this book, I've suggested some 300 books worth reading. A knowledgeable librarian can recommend thousands more – and share her enthusiasm for the books.

books to fix her bike, or join in an Eric Wilson mystery, or find a joke to tell her friends. At the same time, your child's recognition vocabulary will multiply from the 3,000 easy words most grade three students have mastered to the 70,000 to 100,000 word recognition vocabulary a high school student needs. So long as reading is encouraged, this growth will take place on its own.

Stage Five: Critical Judgement

The last step in developing young readers doesn't usually occur until adolescence. At this time, your child should learn that there are different ways to read: skimming (speed-reading), studying, and reading for enjoyment. She should learn to position herself towards the text – to be sceptical, or involved, or to read for her own purposes. In short, your child should learn to read as an adult does.

Children in elementary school usually read just one way – at a single speed, with a single uncritical attitude and a single kind of enthusiasm. They will run from Monica Hughes' *The Keeper of the Isis Light* to *The Diary of Anne Frank* to a Sweet Valley High romance and enjoy each book in turn. They will zip through every book at 150 to 250 words per minute, scarcely taking the time to think about what the author's purpose was, or if they agree or disagree with the text, or why they are reading at all.

But the reading of teenagers should be much more self-aware than that. Before approaching a text, your child should have her own purpose in mind. This novel will be for enjoyment, that poem will be looked at for technique, that newspaper editorial will be read for its political bias. Successful readers then choose from an array of reading styles to suit their purposes.

The job of the high school is to help your teenage child develop all these skills. In a good high school, virtually every subject from English to history to physical education should teach your child important skills in reading and thinking.

As a parent, you can support these more sophisticated skills by talking about your child's reading. Your child might not be aware that virtually every newspaper has a political slant. But you can talk about it. Your teenager may think that Stephen King is a better writer than John Irving. You should talk about such critical judgements. Your daughter might be incredibly cynical about TV commercials, but quite gullible when reading an interview with a rock star. Your experience in the larger world can help make sense of what your teenager is reading – and give you a chance to connect to her world.

The joy of reading with our children doesn't stop as they, and we, get older; it simply changes. At this last stage, you won't be reading out loud much, you'll be talking about what's read. Ironically, this was also the first stage, back with those wordless picture books when your child was an infant. Your family reading will have come full circle.

The Danger Times

Unfortunately, not every child will move successfully through all the stages of learning to read. There are pitfalls in the process that can virtually stop your child's reading development in its tracks. According to research, the two biggest danger times occur around grade four and grade nine.

Between a quarter and a third of children in school begin losing interest in reading sometime around grade four. The problem is not one of reading skills, which most children have mastered in the primary years. The problem – which affects more boys than girls – seems to be one of interest.

Why? Researchers haven't given us an answer yet, but teachers have ventured some guesses. By grade four, most children are quite competent at

Parent-to-Parent
Starting Late

"I didn't read a book – an entire book – until I was twelve years old. Then I won a book in a newspaper contest, the Junior Press Club. I guess I was so thrilled at winning a book that I decided to read it all the way through. I tried it, and I liked it.

"For me, part of the joy of reading to my children is that it gives me a chance to read all those books I missed as a kid. I guess I'm still catching up."

– Bryan Prince, Hamilton, Ontario

Words and more words . . .

- Total number of words in English: 500,000 (excludes scientific and technical terms)

- Number of words in German; Italian: 125,000; 170,000

- English words recognized by the average Canadian adult: 125,000

- Words used in the works of Shakespeare: 30,000

- Words used in 3 hours of prime-time TV: 7,000

- Words recognized orally by a child entering school: 6,000

- Words ordinarily recognized "by sight" by the end of grade 3: 3,000

reading for themselves – so parents stop reading with them. Without parental reinforcement, the *value* of reading goes down in the child's eyes. And reading can be stalled. What's more, children in grades four and five have just enough independence to hang out with friends and to play without adult supervision. Unless some time for reading is preserved, it can be lost in the frantic pace of visiting friends, watching TV, playing tag, practising ballet, and doing math homework.

American researchers have suggested that the root of the problem goes deeper. They feel that the conversation in some families does not support either the advanced vocabulary or the more sophisticated thinking skills required by readers after grade four. Some children have literally never heard the words or ideas they are being asked to read in books. As a result, reading becomes more and more frustrating.

Even in Canada, a number of educators are admitting that their own reading programs lose emphasis starting in grade four. When "reading" turns to "language arts," the emphasis often shifts to writing – as if the job of teaching reading were somehow complete.

The message for parents is clear. You must continue to encourage reading at home through the crucial grade four/five/six period or your child may not develop the sophisticated reading skills she needs. The readers who check out at grade four are barely reading at a grade six level when they enter high school. They won't be ready to face the sophisticated reading demands of secondary school.

The second major danger time is around grade nine. That is when teachers have noted a marked decline in the amount of time many students spend reading for pleasure. The decline frequently begins in grade seven or eight and continues through grade eleven. By that time, only twenty percent of high school students continue to read avidly for themselves. Some fifty-five percent will do little more than the minimal outside reading required for school. And a quarter of our teenagers will hardly bother to read at all.

There are many explanations for this teenage fallow period. Certainly there are many competing demands on the free time of adolescents. Teenagers' attention can become centred on themselves, their social life, or the consumer products pitched at them in the media. Books can seem irrelevent – aimed at either children or adults – failing to deal with teenage concerns. And the rebellious attitude of some teenagers can be aimed not just at parents and schools but at books and reading.

Yet, despite all this, your child can continue to be a reader throughout the teenage years – and will certainly be better off for doing so. You can keep talking about your teenager's reading, keep helping her to add to her library, keep enough rules on the household so that TV and the stereo don't take over her free time. In Chapters 8 and 10, I'll offer a number of other suggestions to help you keep your child reading despite adolescent angst and distraction.

With enough encouragement and support at home, you can help your child through the two big danger times. The reward, for both of you, will be an adult who has become a reader for life.

Where Books Stand

According to Statistics Canada, this is what Canadians spent on various items in 1989/90:

Lamps and lampshades: $3.3 billion
Cosmetics and perfumes: $2.7 billion
Books in bookstores: $275 million
Dolls and stuffed animals: $222 million
Running shoes: $64 million
Hardcover books in English: $40.6 million
Rollerskating: $13.8 million

CHAPTER 3

Parents and the School

Your child's school is your most important partner in encouraging your child to become a reader for life. The teachers at that school will develop lessons with phonics exercises and "whole language" books in the early grades. They'll push for vocabulary development and comprehension skills to match the more sophisticated reading of the middle grades. And the teachers will do their best to keep your child reading and thinking about literature in senior elementary grades and high school. Most teachers will try to meet your child's individual needs, while also trying to meet demands from the province, the school board, the principal, and twenty-five other children who *all* have pressing needs – from wanting to feed the gerbils to surviving a messy divorce at home.

Amazingly, the teachers will do a pretty good job in the midst of all this.

But learning to read – and learning to love reading – requires more than just teachers who do a pretty good job. Reading is so important that our children need excellent instruction in reading and writing fundamentals. They need schools that spur creativity and a sense of excitement

31

about reading. They need school boards and districts that set reading as a top priority and give it the time, the books and the money that it requires.

An Excellent School Reading Program

An excellent school reading program involves commitment, energy and imagination. It is linked to every subject area, but especially to writing, speaking, and dramatic arts. It is eclectic: an excellent reading program isn't limited to phonics, or look-say or whole language philosophy; it draws from all these approaches. An excellent reading program is always organized and structured to make sure that both reading and reading instruction are taking place. But it makes reading fun, not just work. It makes responding to books a creative endeavour, not drudgery.

In Chapters 4 to 12, I'll discuss excellent programs at specific grade levels and for special situations. But first let me suggest three ideas to promote reading for an entire school:

- No school-based approach to encourage reading works better than USSR (Universal, Silent, Structured Reading), sometimes called SQUIRT (Sustained, Quiet, UnInterrupted Reading Time). In this approach, everybody from kindergartners to custodians takes time out from classes and work to read for fifteen minutes a day.

- No single place at school is more important in developing reading than the school library. The library must always be open, staffed, inviting and full of books.

- No program works better for helping weak readers than a buddy system in which senior students read with junior ones, adult volunteers with students who are having the most trouble in reading.

The teachers at an excellent school know that these programs and the attitudes they represent are as important as any particular technique used in any given classroom.

The Parents' Role

The way you deal with your child's school and your child's teachers will depend on the kind of job they are already doing. If the school and teacher are excellent, you can content yourself with being a quiet partner in boosting your child's reading. But if the school or teacher is less than excellent, your position must be more aggressive – sometimes even adversarial – to get the kind of education your child deserves.

Here are thumbnail portraits of three schools and three teachers as you and I would see them on a visit. They are, incidentally, three real schools and three composite teachers from the hundreds I've visited over the past few years. One of them will probably resemble the school your child attends or the teacher he has this year:

School A

School A is a small elementary school with 300 students, drawing half its kids from farms and half from a nearby subdivision. It's 9:45 AM. Walk inside the doors and the principal's office is to the right. But the principal isn't in his office, he's off judging a contest in the kindergarten classroom. The library down the hall isn't elaborate – just two connected classrooms – but the place is full of kids working on projects. There are books everywhere and comfortable couches to sit and read. And there are staff – a full-time librarian, a part-time library/media technician, and two parent volunteers.

Walk down the halls and you'll see photographs of kids everywhere, as if every student in the school has won some kind of award. You have to step around kids as you walk because

The Current Buzz Words in Reading

- Basal readers: books of gradually increasing difficulty based on increasingly complex phonic rules, like the famous Dick and Jane series. Currently fading.

- Whole language: a means of teaching reading using children's literature instead of basal readers, with an attempt to integrate reading, language, and writing. Currently in.

- Phonics: the traditional means of teaching reading by sounding out unfamiliar words. Currently fading.

- Look-say: a means of teaching reading without phonics, whereby students are taught to recognize entire words at one glance. Currently out.

- Resource centre: the school library, especially if it's equipped with computers, tape listening centres, or audio visual equipment. Currently in.

- Resource teacher: not the librarian, but a specially trained teacher who assists students with learning problems. Usually these are special education teachers. Currently in.

An Excellent School Reading Program

Here are some things an excellent school reading program does:

• It sets aside time for reading every day.

• It involves the whole school in reading, sometimes with SQUIRT (Sustained, Quiet, UnInterrupted Reading Time) that includes teachers, students, and custodians.

• It makes effective use of the school library.

• It has novels and magazines in every classroom to augment the library.

• At the primary level, it uses a number of teaching approaches: phonics, whole word or look-say, whole language.

• It uses reading and writing as part of every subject from math to geography.

• It has resource teachers to help students who are having trouble reading.

• It uses parent volunteers and older students as reading buddies to help junior readers.

• It encourages kids to respond to their reading through drama, or art, or writing, not simply to answer set questions.

so many of them are working on the floors, or measuring locker heights, or otherwise using the hallway as if it were an extension of the classroom.

Walk into room 224 and you'll find it noisy. Teacher A has arranged the students in groups of three or four. All of them are working on an art and drama project connected to an author's visit later in the week. On the walls are the kids' own novels, carefully bound with wallpaper covers and a very professional "about the author" page, including the information that Jenny Ferrara, age eleven, has two cats, Muffy and Smith.

Teacher A, dressed in jeans and boots for an afternoon field trip to a nearby conservation area, hasn't noticed you because she's too busy with one of the groups. But everyone notices a bell that sounds at 10:00. It's reading time. The groups disband. Students grab books or magazines from their desks, then slump against the walls or into chairs and begin to read. It's quiet. The teacher is reading, too, her boots propped up on a file cabinet. Out in the hall, the custodian is reading a John Le Carre novel. Fifteen minutes later, it's back to regular lessons, even though half the kids groan when they have to put their books away.

School B

School B is a sprawling junior high school with an enrolment pushing 1,000. The school draws its students from six elementary schools, some as far as eighty kilometres away. There is a string of portable classrooms on part of the school yard.

It's 11:30 AM – almost lunch – and there's a lot of noise pouring from classrooms into the halls, even though no one is in sight. The halls themselves are undecorated, walls of lockers stretching out their full length. There is dust on the trophies in the display cabinet.

Walk down the hall and peek into the library. It's a good-sized room with probably 3,000 books

– hardcovers from the time the school was built and racks of newer paperbacks. There are two computers, one of which is out of order, and a number of tables and study carrels, some of them occupied. The librarian is busy trying to convince a grade eight teacher that maybe she should use a new book by Canadian writer William Bell instead of doing *Shane* for the fifteenth year.

Keep walking down the hall and turn into classroom 113. The desks are in neat rows, though the kids are sprawled all over. The kids in this grade seven class are watching Teacher B as he passes out the comprehension questions on a short story called "The Monkey's Paw" by W.W. Jacobs. Most of the kids have read the story, except for two kids at the back of the room who never read anything. Teacher B explains that he used to try more elaborate lessons with the kids – dramatizing stories, interviewing characters in books, even shooting videos instead of doing written book reports. But now he's emphasizing writing, because there's a new provincial initiative and the principal expects the kids' expensive cardboard writing folders to be filled by the end of the year.

Teacher B reminds the students that they have a book report due next week, though most of them haven't started reading a book yet. There just doesn't seem to be time, Teacher B will tell you, to get through the curriculum, do all the paperwork, and still read books.

School C

School C serves a farming area. It's a small school with only 250 students in a reasonably new and clean building.

It's 2:30 PM when you walk into the school. The classroom doors are closed and there are no kids in the halls. There's a sign that orders you to report to the office, but the principal is busy disciplining a kid, and the secretary is too busy to notice you.

Help Needed

Your child's school needs help when . . .

- the school library has only a handful of books or is closed;

- reading instruction is done only through phonics or look-say, or without any structure;

- reading is done only one period a day, and it's work;

- the principal or teacher says, "Personally, I don't have time to read";

- your child comes home every day with no homework, no book to read, and no excitement about school;

- you ask your child, "What are you reading in school these days," and she says, "Nothing," and you say, "Come on, you must be reading something," and she repeats, "Nothing" and means it.

Instead of waiting, you head down the hall, past the library with its handful of books. The teacher-librarian comes in every other day now, due to budget cutbacks, but there's a parent volunteer at her desk. If you look through the collection, you won't find many books for the grade seven and eight kids because the teacher-librarian likes to avoid controversy. She heard about the trouble a local high school had with the swear words in John Steinbeck's *Of Mice and Men*, so you won't find even a *damn* in any of the books in her library.

Walk into the grade five classroom of Teacher C, and everything is very orderly. You could hear a pin drop as the kids work, warily eyeing the teacher who sits at her desk at the front of the room. The students are looking up vocabulary words in dictionaries to complete definitions demanded by their spelling text. When the students do "reading" at 9:15 AM tomorrow, the story will be from a textbook with questions at the end of the selection.

Reading in Teacher C's classroom is frequently out loud, even though a third of the kids get nervous and make a lot mistakes when they're called upon. The good readers are forbidden to laugh at the weak readers, but the kids still know. Most of the weak readers will tell you that they hate reading, but that may just mean they're embarrassed to read out loud.

Teacher C doesn't feel there is much she can do about the attitude of some of the kids. With thirty-two kids in the classroom, she sometimes feels buried under the marking load. And the school district isn't providing any help, because the once-a-week reading specialists were cut with the last budget crunch.

Teacher C hasn't heard of reading buddies, or quiet reading time, and doesn't much like this whole language idea because it's so airy-fairy. She believes in good old oral reading from the approved textbook. She likes vocabulary study with dictionaries and grammar sheets from a workbook because that's what worked for her. Maybe it would still work, if the kids weren't so "difficult" these days.

Virtually all of Canada's 14,000 schools fall into the range I've described above. We have a few schools where the level of experimentation, and excitement, and cooperation will strike you within minutes. We have a great many schools where the school is good enough and teachers are trying, but something is missing – staff morale, money for books and equipment, or a dynamic principal. Sadly, we have the schools in every province where rigid administrations or lack-lustre teachers have eliminated any excitement or joy that children have the right to expect. As a visitor, these schools appal me: they deaden the joy of learning for our children.

Observe Your Child's School and Classroom

The first step in working with your child's school is to observe, much as I have done in the visits I just described. Too many parents worry that they don't belong in the school, or they feel awkward talking to teachers or stepping into the halls. But your taxes built the school and pay teacher salaries – and you've entrusted your own child to their care. Surely, *you*, even more than I, have the right to know what's going on at your child's school.

So nose around. Drop in to chat with the principal – you don't really need an appointment, though it's wise to call ahead. Say that you're interested in the school reading program. A good principal will be pleased to talk about what her school is doing. On your way out, check out the hall displays, look around the library, chat with the custodian or the secretary at the front desk. You'll form an immediate impression about the "feel" of the school.

Then use the school's parents' night to find out about your child's teacher and classroom. The first parents' night is usually sometime before

A Good School Library

A good school library should do much more than provide books to kids once a week.

- The school librarian should be a curriculum leader, actively suggesting new books to other teachers.

- A good school library reaches out to children's homes – sometimes lending one book to be read by the child, a second book to be read by a parent.

- The school library should be a project centre with everything from rulers and glue sticks to magazines that can be cut up for pictures.

- School libraries ought to have more than books – computers, encyclopedias on CD ROM, audio centres for foreign language study, audio and video tapes, talking books, film strips.

- The school librarian frequently organizes volunteers or co-ordinates the reading-buddy program.

- A good school librarian knows every child and has some sense of what each child likes to read.

- A good library always provides a quiet, comfortable corner for reading.

Hallowe'en. This initial visit is more important than your sales meeting or the euchre club or anything else you might prefer to do. Always go to the first meet-the-teacher night. It's vital for your child and his teacher to know you support his education. And it's important for you to know what's going on.

Look around the classroom. Is it bright, lively, full of displays of the kids' work? Is there a classroom library? Is there a computer, science equipment, a reading corner? Is your child's work organized into a folder or on display?

Then talk to the teacher. What books does he use for the reading program? How often does the class go to the school library? Are there reading buddies, drama exercises, projects coming up, field trips planned? How much homework does the teacher expect? How much outside reading? Is there anything you can do to help on field trip days or as a volunteer?

Always keep your ears open to that third great source of information – your child. When you ask, "What did you do at school today?" try to get past the immediate "Nothing" to find out what really happened. What is your child reading? How does he feel about his teacher? How does he talk about school – with excitement or with boredom? Often the tone of kids talking about their school and their teacher will tell you more than the words they use. Listen.

Then use this book. Check the margin to see how many components of a top-level reading program are present in your school. Check in the later chapters for information on what a school should be doing in the specific grades for your child. Once you've made a reasonably solid judgement on how good your child's school is, you'll be ready to decide what to do next.

If You're Lucky: An "A" School, An "A" Teacher

In my travels, I've run across dozens of "A" schools, from small schools in farming communities to sprawling, multicultural inner-city

Five Questions for Parents' Night

Q: What books or textbooks do you use in language arts? May I look through one?

Q: What homework should my child expect? Would it be okay for me to offer my child some help?

Q: How often does the class visit the library to get books? Can my child bring these books home?

Q: Do you have any special activities going on this year? A young authors' workshop? A special drama performance? Field trips?

Q: How may I help?

schools, from wealthy private schools to dirt-poor alternative schools. There is no single system that produces a fine school. Instead, it takes some combination of a dynamic principal, committed teachers, community support, and good luck. If your child is in an "A" school, with an "A" teacher, your job is to support and encourage what's going on. Here are some ways to do that:

- Praise the teacher. A note of thanks or appreciation often makes a difficult job worthwhile. Some years ago, I chaired an organization for student debating which involved twenty-four schools and 300 kids. This bit of volunteer work used up some twenty hours a month of my time, and after two years and one particularly exhausting tournament, I was ready to call it quits. But that night I got a call from a parent who said nothing more than thanks for organizing such an opportunity for his son. It made my evening and kept me in the chair for another year.

- Volunteer your time. An excellent school always makes use of volunteers. That means you. If your days are relatively free, why not tutor reading, or help in the library, or take the kindergarten kids to the zoo? Even if you work every day, the school can still use your help. Join the home and school organization, or the principal's advisory group. Make yourself available for career day or concert night. Let the school and your child's teacher know that you can be counted on.

- Pay attention to your child's schoolwork. Even excellent schools and teachers can't do their job unless you do yours. In twenty years of teaching, I've encountered only a handful of families who interfered too much in their children's education; but I knew thousands who paid virtually no attention to what was going on in school. If you are reading nightly with your child, you will naturally talk about what is being read at school. Keep on asking questions. The older a child gets, the more you'll have to push for answers. Is there a science fair? What project does your daughter have in mind for geography? Does your son want try some of the mental math problems on you? Your interest in schoolwork, like your involvement in reading, gives importance to what happens in school.

- Protect your school. There are many forces in Canada that endanger all our schools – from budget-cutting trustees to self-righteous zealots who would purge libraries of such "dangerous" books as J.D. Salinger's *The Catcher in the Rye*. Your school may need your help just to protect what it already has.

Dealing with "B" Schools and "B" Teachers

The "B" school and "B" teacher are not excellent, but not clearly deficient, either. They simply lack the energy, imagination, and commitment that would lead to real excellence.

You can make up for some of this by effective parenting at home. If you support your child's reading with the three Rs, chances are your child will develop excellent reading skills and learn to love reading on his own. But you'll find it harder to develop home programs to support a weak geography or math teacher. When your child gets older, you'll find it very difficult to help much in calculus or physics. That's why you have to use some of your energy to put on pressure for better education at school. Here are some ways to do that:

Home and School

For help to set up a home and school group, contact one of these organizations:

- British Columbia Confederation of Parent Advisory Councils
#1540-1185 W. Georgia Street
Vancouver, B.C. V6E 4E6
(604) 687-4433; Fax (604) 687-4488

- Alberta Federation of Home and School Associations
#312-11010-142 Street
Edmonton, Alberta T5N 2R1
(403) 454-9867; Fax (403) 455-6481

- Saskatchewan Federation of Home and School Associations
221 Cumberland Avenue North
Saskatoon, Saskatchewan S7N 1M3
(306) 933-5723

- Home and School and Parent-Teacher Federation of Manitoba
Box 158, 905 Corydon Avenue
Winnipeg, Manitoba, R3M 3S7
(204) 489-7741

- Ontario Federation of Home and School Associations
252 Bloor Street West, Suite 12-200
Toronto, Ontario M5S 1V5
(416) 924-7491; Fax (416) 924-5354

- Use the ideas in this book to promote a strong school reading program. There are no particularly radical ideas here, so a comment such as "I was reading a book that says every school should have a silent reading time" ought to get at least a few heads nodding in agreement. Or you might want to read some of the books listed in my Notes on Sources about the effective schools movement. In my experience, most "B" schools want to be better; they just haven't figured out how yet.

- Organize with other parents. As an individual or couple, you don't have much clout. As part of the principal's advisory group, or the music parents association, or the home and school, you speak with greater authority. Good principals are always seeking out input from parents on everything from report card design to attendance procedures. As part of an organization, your voice will be heard.

  Parent organizations often serve another useful function: raising cash for special projects. When Elizabeth Cooney in Toronto felt her kids' separate school needed extra cash to buy books, schools supplies, and computers, she organized parents to sell chocolate bars and raffle tickets. While I hate to see parents' energies devoted entirely to fund-raising – after all, that's what school boards are for – sometimes a little extra money will buy those frills that make school an exciting place to learn.

- Seek out the excellent teachers. Every ordinary school has some quite extraordinary teachers. In high school, with some careful course choices and a little quiet nudging, your child can often arrange for classes with the very best teachers. Many elementary schools have two or three

- Quebec Federation of Home and School Associations
  3285 Cavendish Boulevard, Suite 562
  Montreal, Quebec H4B 2L9
  (519) 481-5619

- New Brunswick Federation
  c/o 8 Teesdale Street,
  Moncton, New Brunswick E1A 5K5
  (506) 855-9556

- Le Regroupement Foyer-Ecole du Nouveau-Brunswick Inc.
  c/o 187 rue Angers
  St-Basile, New Brunswick E0L 1H0
  (506) 735-5900

- Nova Scotia Federation of Home and School Associations
  209-515 Prince Street
  Truro, Nova Scotia B2N 1E8
  (902) 895-0664

- Prince Edward Island Federation of Home & School Associations
  P.O. Box 1012
  Charlottetown, P.E.I. C1A 7M4
  (902) 895-0664

- Newfoundland & Labrador Federation of Home & School & Parent-Teacher Associations
  P.O. Box 13911, St. John's
  Newfoundland A1B 4G7
  (709) 739-4830

teachers at each grade level. If you can determine from friends and neighbours which teacher is superior, try to get your child into her class by speaking candidly with the principal.

Then back up those excellent teachers when they come up with an exciting initiative for the school. Sometimes a handful of dynamic staff members can make a school soar despite a lack-lustre principal.

Bad News: The "C" School and "C" Teacher

These are the most discouraging schools to deal with. The administration and staff are closed off and unfriendly. The school or classroom atmosphere is rigid, boring, or disorganized almost to the point of chaos. Your child suddenly doesn't want to go to school, or wakes up late again and again, or develops mysterious ailments that seem to go away as soon as you say, "Okay, you can stay home today."

The solutions here come down to three:

- First, you can take your kids out of school and do what you can as a "home schooler." This route takes a tremendous commitment of time and energy and is rarely possible beyond elementary school. Formal application must be made to your provincial Ministry or Department of Education. Course outlines are kept on file and provincial guidelines must be followed. No wonder only a tiny fraction of Canadian children are home-schooled.

- Second, you can try to move your family or your child. In the United States, schools and school budgets vary tremendously from state to state, county to county. Parents there sometimes move the whole household just to find a good school for their children. In Canada, schools are much more uniform because school finance is a provincial jurisdiction. It's unlikely that a move from inner city to suburb, or town to town will have much effect on the quality of your child's school. Nonetheless, if your child has ended up in a poor school and your efforts to work with the principal and teachers have failed, it might well be best to move your child to a different school. Many urban school systems permit school-to-school moves for any valid reason, from "I want to take Latin" to "My daughter is unhappy here." A supportive teacher can tell you what kind of reason is likely to work with your school system. In some provinces you can transfer to a competing school system – separate, public, or private – which might have a better school nearby for your child.

• Third, you can put pressure on an inadequate school or teacher to improve. That's what the rest of this chapter is all about.

How To Speak with Your Child's Teacher

If the problems you observe are at the classroom level, the place to start is with the teacher. Twice a year, you'll be invited into the school to speak with your child's teacher. This doesn't mean you may not go in any other time – or twice a month if you wanted to – but twice a year you'll be invited to do so. Always attend. Your child's education is worth the effort.

Be charming but firm. You never want to be in the position of making the teacher feel defensive – that doesn't make for change. Try to understand the teacher's side: "Yes, it must be difficult with thirty children in the class . . . . I can understand how wrangy my son can get." Even excellent teachers can have personal problems, or especially difficult classes, or an

What Works

Jeanne Chall's 1990 study on what works and doesn't work in teaching reading:

What works:
- reading books that challenge the student,
- structure in the classroom and regular attendance by students,
- regular homework for students,
- "literacy environment" in classroom and use of school library.

What doesn't work:
- vocabulary study unrelated to reading,
- oral reading by students in class,
- emphasis on teacher-directed lessons.

administration that doesn't support what they would like to do.

But always have your own agenda. You have already made your observations. Before you go in for the interview, you should have a good idea what's needed. You want a reading program with a wide range of books. Maybe you want some stimulating classroom discussion and activities, not just answering questions on page 34. Maybe you want writing tied to reading, and spelling from what the kids are reading, and some creative writing in the classroom. Whatever you'd like to have happen, make your expectations clear. Don't let the teacher suggest that problems in instruction are the result of bad or stupid kids. More often classroom problems have to do with lifeless teaching.

Offer ideas. Your son's teacher may not know that most provinces will fund author visits to schools and classrooms. Your daughter's teacher may not have thought about reading buddies, or visiting the public library once a month, or sending books home to be read with the parent. Since you know about these ideas, suggest them.

Follow through. It is impossible to emphasize enough the importance of follow-through. Your last comment to a teacher should always be, "I'll phone you in two weeks to see how all this is coming along." Then do it. The teacher should return your call. If not, call again and call the principal – "I haven't been able to get in touch with Mrs. Martin. Maybe you could help."

Keep a record of your visits, your calls, and what was said. The date and a few notes are all you need. If push does come to shove, it's far better to tell the principal that you spoke with Mrs. Martin on September 23, October 4, 9, and 15, than to mumble, "Well, I talked to her a couple of times."

Parents are always afraid that any aggressiveness they show towards a teacher will be taken out on their child. In my experience, that's rarely the case. Usually, your child will get kid-glove treatment because you have shown so much interest. Even better, you may be able to make real changes in what happens in your child's classroom.

When Push Comes to Shove

The keys to making lasting changes in your child's school or classroom are persistence and organization. I have seen at least two persistent parents, bothered by what was happening in their local schools, go from pestering their boards and being labelled as "wackos" to become a school trustee in one case and a member of the legislature in the other. It is amazing how power makes that "wacko" label just disappear.

You can be just as successful. What you need is a calm, persistent approach, a way to organize yourself and other parents and some knowledge of how power works in the schools.

Teachers are at the low end of the power scale. They have some control over how they teach, but little say over what they teach, or the books they use, or the size of their classes, or the tone of their schools. Teachers who teach poorly can be helped or prodded by their principals. Only very new teachers can easily be fired for incompetence. Teachers close to retirement might be safe even from forced transfer. Nonetheless, you have every right to demand up-to-date and effective instruction from a professional who makes $30,000 to $60,000 a year.

Principals have differing levels of power, depending on their board or district and the community where they teach. In the old days, a teacher could be dismissed by a principal for failing to shine his shoes. These days, teachers' unions and federations make that impossible. But principals still have substantial powers in their schools: they distribute money, approve field trips, transfer staff, and do much to set the tone and keep up the morale in their school.

The Power Chart

School power starts at the top (provincial level) and trickles down. As a parent, you have to start at the bottom and pester your way up.

- Your provincial ministry or department of education
- Your local elected board of education trustees
- Superintendents of your school board or division
- Subject supervisors/consultants – especially in English, reading and libraries
- The principal of your child's school
- The teacher of your child's class
- You
- Your child

Teachers on Literacy

The Canadian Teachers' Federation surveyed 14,000 teachers to get their views on literacy in 1989–90. Here are some findings:

- Of secondary teachers who saw a change in the "quality of students' literacy" over the previous ten years, 62 percent thought it was lower; 38 percent thought it had improved.

- Primary teachers (grades kindergarten to three) thought that 19 percent of their students had some literacy problems; 10 percent had "critical difficulties." By grades four to six, teachers thought 21 percent of their students had some literacy problems; 15 percent were critical.

- Factors that teachers thought hurt student literacy: family instability, lack of stimulation at home, lack of parental support and encouragement, low value placed on literacy in the home, student suffers from low self-esteem, student is shy or withdrawn, student has behavioural problems.

Effective principals may plead powerlessness, but the good ones find ways to get the staff they want and push forward the programs they believe in. If you can get the principal on your side, much can be done to change what happens in your child's school.

Consultants, supervisors, and superintendents have been promoted from classrooms and schools to oversee whole subject areas or groups of schools. They have power based on elaborate flow charts at your board or district. Superintendents are drawn from the ranks of principals either for educational leadership or "fire-fighting" skills. You can assume the educational leaders will be on your side; just watch out that you don't get hosed by the superintendent assigned to handle parental brushfires. None of these individuals has much power in your son's classroom, but a phone call to the right one can put pressure on a foot-dragging principal.

School boards and districts are usually controlled by elected officials called trustees. It is at this level that local budgets are set and program emphasis is determined. If libraries are underfunded while football teams ride around in chauffeured limos, then your local school board or district has its values backwards. Work to turf out the offending trustees by electing people who support serious education.

A good school trustee can be quite helpful in adding muscle to your dealings with a school principal. While the trustees' role is technically advisory, their voices still carry a fair deal of weight. If push comes to shove, try to get one or more trustees on your side.

Your provincial ministry or department of education is the place where the power really sits – but is rarely used. The ministry sets goals, doles out money, and sometimes creates programs in the schools. If your school decides it wants to add 100 books to its library, that's three bake sales for the home and school association and it's still only books for one school. If your provincial ministry or department of education decides that kids should be reading more – that school libraries are essential in every school – then one piece of legislation will send millions of dollars moving in that direction. Remember: the money spent building a kilometre of two-lane highway would provide more than 80,000 paperback books for the school libraries in your province. Keep that in mind when you vote.

Parents should understand the levers of power in school systems just in case they have to use them. It's unlikely your child will be in a terrible school, or have three poor teachers in a row. But you can't afford to stand by if you feel the school or teachers are unsatisfactory. In this book, I've suggested ways for you to encourage and support your child's reading, but it is not your job to *teach* reading. That's the school's job. You should be able to rely on the school to do that teaching in an organized, effective and exciting way. Don't settle for less.

CHAPTER 4

Getting Started:
Infancy to Age Five

Your two-year-old sits on your lap, pointing at pictures in a book which she looks at again and again, calling out the names of the animals, telling you what's going to happen on the next page. This is a wonderful part of being a parent, but is it reading?

Of course it is. For too many years we have had a very narrow view of reading, one that confuses the lifelong process of learning to read with the simple decoding we learn around age six and seven.

We now know that the toddler who experiences language and stories through books is the child who will find it easy to read for herself later on. The child who doesn't hear our language, who isn't told stories, and who doesn't have the opportunity to look at books in childhood will be at a disadvantage for the rest of her life.

So "infant reading" must begin early. We will never fully know how much an infant sees, or hears, or understands. We suspect that babies can focus only at close distances, and that they hear higher-pitched voices better than lower ones, and that they are busy constructing in their

Books for Babies

If you read to your baby, your baby will want to read to herself — or at least pretend to. Tough treatment requires a sturdy book with heavy cardboard pages. Try these:

Debbie Bailey and Susan Juszar, *My Dad.* (Annick, 1991) Photos tell the story about this important person in a baby's life. Part of a series.

Dick Bruna, *Miffy* (Methuen, 1964) and many other titles. Bruna's simple illustrations were all the rage a few years ago. Babies still love them.

Micheline Chartrand and Helene Desputeaux, *Lollipop's Room* and other Lollipop books (Crowell, 1976, etc.). Illustrations show baby Lollipop's emotions. In regular and tiny-hand editions.

Richard Thompson and Eugenie Fernandes, *Effie's Bath* (Annick, 1989). Very bold illustrations show an important daily ritual for your baby.

Barbara Reid, *Zoe's Sunny Day* (Scholastic, 1991). Part of a series about Zoe, a lively preschooler. The Plasticine illustrations contain much to talk about.

minds the universe that surrounds them. We know they need closeness and cuddling and love.

What better way to meet all these needs than by "infant reading" to a baby as young as three weeks old.

I've been using the expression "infant reading" instead of "reading" because the activity we do with infants bears as much resemblance to later reading as T-ball does to the World Series. Of course, T-ball is good for kids and will likely be the start for our next generation of baseball players. Just so, early infant reading develops an attitude towards books and print that is important for reading later on.

Infant reading doesn't have that much to do with the actual words on the page; it has more to do with playing and talking, singing and laughing, observing and exploring, tickling and having fun together. For tiny infants, there are special books with waterproof vinyl pages that can be propped up on the changing table, left in the crib, or even set to float in the bathtub. While you can't very well sit down and read with your infant for long periods of time as you would with an older child, you can still encourage infant reading by making sure there are books in your child's crib or playpen or out on the floor. When your baby looks at a book out of curiosity, you can use that interest to talk about the pictures, to read the simple text, or to have fun by singing, clapping, or making funny sounds.

Infants look at books with bursts of intense concentration. That's when you should do infant reading with your child. The best books for infants have big, simple shapes which your baby will scrutinize for a few minutes while you read or talk or explain. Then the baby will turn away, because this early experience of reading is a very intense one. Turning away from the book is also a part of reading, part of your baby's discovery that books are a special part of her world.

For three chapters now, I've been talking about reading as an attitude more than a set of skills.

Attitudes start early. The one-year-old baby who wants to eat her cloth book about bears is busy exploring the world of print. Eating for a baby is part of her process of understanding the world. To understand the idea of "book," she must eat it, tear it, crunch it, and ignore it – all at the same time she learns that a book is something to be encountered visually. Obviously, some first books will be damaged as they're touched and manipulated by your child. Just keep the expensive illustrated hardcover books out of the playpen. They're for you and your baby to read together at other times in order for books to become part of your relationship with each other.

Getting into Stories

Sometime between eighteen and thirty months, a baby's language skills develop dramatically. Just as crawling turns to walking, so babbling turns to talking. At this stage, infant reading becomes much closer to ordinary reading. Current research says that your child is busy at this point creating stories in her own mind – to understand herself, the spot of sunlight on the floor, her teddy bear. This is the time when books become much more than shapes and sounds for her. They begin to convey both language and story.

The key for this change lies in favourite books. In dealing with young children, I cannot overemphasize the importance of letting children select their favourites from a large number of books. Then read those favourite books together with your child again and again.

Marcia Baghban, the author of *Our Daughter Learns to Read and Write*, offers a remarkable study of the way her daughter, Gita, picked up language skills from birth to age three. As part of her graduate work at Indiana University, she tape-recorded many of their times reading together. Here's a transcript that shows the kind of reading Gita was doing at twenty-four months:

Easy on the Budget

A good children's book can be quite expensive, though never as much as a pair of jeans or a good dinner out. Some publishers offer bargain-basement prices on books for young children.

- Golden Books. Mass-produced in the United States with more than 600 titles now, some of these inexpensive hardcover books have become classics:
  The Little Red Caboose
  Little Toot
  Animal Daddies and My Daddy
  Dumbo
  Little Red Riding Hood

- Annikins. There are now thirty-three of these very short, very small books produced in Canada and sold by the millions. Here are five of the best:
  Allen Morgan, *Matthew and the Midnight Tow Truck*
  Robert Munsch, *Mud Puddle*
  Kathy Stinson, *Big or Little*
  Lesley Simpson, *The Hug*
  Roger Paré, *A Friend Like You*

MOM: How about your book about Winnie-the-Pooh? Do you think you can read this yourself.

GITA: No, Mommy. You. You.

MOM: O.K. Let's try this book. Who's this book about?

GITA: Winnie Pooh.

MOM: Right. (reads) *Winnie-the-Pooh lives in a house in the forest. Here is Pooh Bear –*

GITA: Pooh Bear.

MOM: *– with his friend Christopher Robin. They are reading a funny story.*

GITA: Story.

MOM: Um hum. (reading) *Shy Piglet is afraid of his own shadow. There's nothing Pooh likes better than eating honey with piglet.* (to Gita) Where's the honey?

GITA: (Points to honey pot.) Honey.

MOM: Who's this?

GITA: Tiger.

MOM: Right. (reading) *Tigger is Pooh's bouncy friend. And Owl is Pooh's knowing friend. He explains things to Pooh.*

GITA: E-ore. E-ore.

MOM: Right. (reading) *Eyeore is a gloomy friend.* (to Gita) He's a donkey, see?

GITA: Donkey.

MOM: (reading) *Now Eyeore is happy. He's glad to see Winnie-the-Pooh. Winnie-the-Pooh is happy to see Eyeore.*

GITA: Winnie Pooh happy. Susie happy. Lassie happy. Mommy happy. Baba happy.

Looking at this conversation carefully, you can see how the favourite book brings about the entire exchange. Gita is responding to a story and characters she already knows. Sometimes she is predicting the next picture or section in the book. Sometimes she is echoing her mother's words. Sometimes she is using the model of the story to understand her own world and to express her own experience.

Of course, young children also enjoy new and different books, but it is in repeated reading of favourite books that real gains are made in understanding stories and language. After twenty readings of *Each Peach Pear Plum* by Janet and Allan Ahlberg or *The Cat In the Hat* by Dr. Seuss or *The New Baby Calf* by Edith Chase and Barbara Reid, you'll desperately want to move on to another book. But your child will still be taking in the language, the pictures, the ideas and the experience of reading that favourite book. For her sake, keep reading it.

One of the wonderful things about good children's books is that they are often so interesting to adults. Something in us responds, as we read, to the kinds of stories that children also love. Timeless stories ranging from *Three Little Pigs* to Robert Munsch's *Thomas' Snowsuit* will find a resonant chord that makes reading fun for us, too.

It is our interest and attention that makes reading such a wonderful experience for young children. If you count the words in Marcia Baghban's reading to her daughter, you'll find that only half of what's spoken is actually reading. The other half is explaining, asking, identifying and exploring. These aren't just activities that go along with reading – they are *part* of reading. If you take too much time with the text and ignore all the rest, then the process of reading will be dry and lifeless. Reading time should always be full of talk and play, even if that has little obvious connection to the story.

To maintain your own interest – and expand your child's experience with books – it's

Reading Aloud – Any Questions?

Researchers at the University of Houston tape-recorded 147 hours of parents reading with young children aged three to five. They found that girls in their sample tended to ask more questions than boys, but all children were curious about pictures, the story, and word meaning – in that order.

How many questions? On average, the children asked one question every 2.26 minutes.

Books by Mail

If there are no bookstores in your area, a good way to get new books for your child is to sign up for a children's book club. Try these:

> Doubleday Children's Book Club
> 105 Bond Street
> Toronto, Ontario M5B 1Y3

Three books for a dollar, then you have to buy six more books over two years. Mostly hardcover. Bookstore prices. A few Canadian titles.

> Grolier Book Club
> P.O. Box 1772
> Danbury, Connecticut 06816

The big American book club for kids. Their opening deal is often six or eight classic children's books for five dollars or so. The catch is that two more books simply arrive in your mailbox each month until you cry whoa! Almost no Canadian titles.

important to keep trying to enlarge the field of what's read. Book clubs for young children are an especially good source, since a new book or two appears on your doorstep each month. A weekly trip to the bookstore or library is even better because your range of choice is wider and it turns book selection into an event. Grandparents and other relatives can be encouraged to give books or bring library books when they come to visit. There's always the chance that one of the new books will become a favourite book. In fact, the better the book, the far more likely it is to become a favourite.

Many young children enter day care quite early on. A good day care program should offer much more than just baby-sitting. Part of the daily activities should be reading books. When you are evaluating day care options, look around the home or day care centre for the book-shelf and ask questions about how much time is spent reading. Excellent day care is always an extension of your own parenting – and it should include lots of time reading together.

How To Tell a Good Picture Book

While your child will always pick her own favourite books for herself, the books that are available to her will probably be selected by you and other relatives. These guidelines, based on the experience of parents, preschool teachers, and librarians, will help you choose good books to buy or bring home from the library.

- The illustrations should be rich enough and detailed enough that you can find extra material to talk about. Some of Mercer Mayer's books have no text at all, so the story becomes what you and your daughter talk about together. The illustrations in Maurice Sendak's *In the Night Kitchen* are so complex and detailed that they would support several stories besides the one in the text.

- The book should be appropriate not just for the child's current age but also for the next year or two. For instance, Dr. Seuss's *Green Eggs and Ham* appeals to babies for its rhythm and rhyme, to three- and four-year-olds because Ham-I-Am is an extension of their own rebelliousness, and to early readers because it's simple enough that they can read it themselves.

- The printed text should be short – a sentence or two per page – but not so short that the pages will be flipped through without discussion. In a picture book, the illustrations are as important as the text (often they are created by separate individuals). In *Lollipop's Room* by Micheline Chartrand the text is very short; in *The Balloon Tree* by Phoebe Gilman the text takes up half a page and is probably at the upper limit of how much your young child will accept before wanting a page turn.

- The text should be predictable, through rhythm, rhyme, or logic, to make it easy for your child to "read" for herself. The early book-babble of babies is mostly based on memorized sounds, many of which are not even understood. Rhyming books like *The Wonderful Pigs of Jillian Jiggs* by Phoebe Gilman or rhythmic books like *Alligator Pie* by Dennis Lee, or books with repeated lines like *Frederick* by Leo Lionni are easy to memorize and easy for your child to respond to, or to recite as you read.

- The story should engage both you and your child. Since reading is sharing, parents will want a book that has some interest for them as well as their child. The sheer beauty of *Whose Mouse Are You?* by Robert Kraus appeals to any

Reading in Daycare

Almost half the young children in Canada will spend some time in day care – and some of that time should be spent reading. According to Nancy Vertolli at Victoria Day Care and Nadia Hall at Mothercraft in Toronto, here's what to expect in a good reading program:

- a book area for children in every room;
- daily reading and story-telling time in small groups or "circles";
- trips to the library for books, films, puppet shows;
- sing-along time with song sheets; read-along time with audio tapes;
- quiet time out with a special book and a volunteer to help reading;
- exploration through books of theme units, from dinosaurs to clowns to family problems.

Six Beautiful Illustrated Books

Phoebe Gilman, *The Balloon Tree*. (North Winds, 1984). An original fairy-tale that looks something like a medieval manuscript.

Dayal Kaur Khalsa, *Sleepers*. (Tundra, 1988). A small going-to-bed story with bright, bold illustrations.

Edith Chase and Barbara Reid, *The New Baby Calf*. (Scholastic, 1984). Wonderful Plasticine illustrations in a story about life on a farm.

Maurice Sendak, *In the Night Kitchen*. (HarperCollins, 1970). Magical dream-story with realistic, anatomically-correct drawings.

Betty Waterton and Joanne Fitzgerald, *Plain Noodles*. (Douglas and McIntyre, 1989). This warm-hearted book speaks to adults about motherhood, but babies love it because there are wonderful babies in the illustrations.

Brian Wildsmith, *Python's Party*. (Oxford, 1987). British whimsy with clever, colourful illustrations of animals.

adult; the magical text of Phoebe Gilman's *Balloon Tree* or the spunky preschooler in *Zoe's Sunny Day* by Barbara Reid appeals to the kid in all of us.

- Nonetheless, the book should be for and about children. In *Lollipop's Room*, the story is about a child's emotions; in *Plain Noodles* by Betty Waterton the appeal of seeing all those babies in illustrations is primarily for other babies. Your child will want to read about other children her own age or slightly older, so she can see herself in the characters of the story.

- The story should suggest some of the great themes – struggle, growth, love, loss – so the book will be useful in the process of growing up. Bruno Bettelheim makes an impressive case in his book *The Uses of Enchantment* that early reading has an important psychological function which requires that it touch honestly on the major tasks and traumas of life. While Grimm's *Fairy Tales* obviously fill the bill, the same might also be said of Robert Munsch's *Thomas' Snowsuit* and its focus on anger and frustration, or P.D. Eastman's *Are You My Mother?* with its tale of loss and search for comfort. A great children's book is never just silly or sweet. It speaks deeply to both parent and child.

- The book should be made well enough to withstand tough use. Heavy board or cloth pages are best for the playpen. Sewn bindings withstand repeated readings. Most cheap paperbacks have what is called a "perfect" binding, which is nothing more than glue. They simply fall apart, fast. The pages of a sewn book are stitched together with thread before the cover is glued on. These are the books that last.

Growing Vocabulary and Understanding

One amazing fact about children is how much reading they can do at a very early age. In North America, a great many children can recognize the word *McDonald's* with the golden arches as early as twenty-four months. By age three, many children have a very practical sight vocabulary of two dozen words or so: *Big Mac, K mart, Cheerios, Stop, Dairy Queen.* As a parent, you may not even be aware that your child is already reading, but she is. The first reading is always based on the words that make sense of the child's world.

The problem with phonics for early readers is that the young mind isn't much interested in theoretical constructions like *choo-boo-too.* While any number of programs exist to teach phonics to young children, the long-term benefit is questionable. You can do phonic drills by the crib, or buy kits that use phonic parts to make snakes or circles, but these exercises are not likely to have much meaning for your child. And there's always the chance that over-zealous instruction will backfire and interfere with your child's love of reading. I suggest you let any formal phonics instruction wait until your child enters school and has a vocabulary and experience base large enough that it will be useful to her.

All you really have to do to start you child reading is read with her. When your child is ready to read for herself – and that will happen at a number of different times in a number of different ways – she'll take over the reading from you. She'll repeat some of your words in that favourite book, then proudly declare that she'll read the next page, or the next word in a line, all by herself. Of course it's as much memory and guesswork as decoding, but it's still reading – just as that first toddling step really is walking. As a parent, you can support and encourage that first step and that first reading, but you can't force them to happen.

Five Classics That Have Stood the Test of Time

Laurent De Brunhoff; *Babar* (Random House, 1940). The characters are dated, but the simple stories and art still appeal.

A.A. Milne, *Winnie-the-Pooh* (Dell, 1926). A delight, both in the original and the Disney-ized versions.

H.A. Rey, *Curious George* (Houghton Mifflin, 1942). The childish monkey is annoying to parents, but works for kids. The originals are much better than the made-for-TV cartoon versions.

Dr. Seuss, *Green Eggs and Ham* (Random House, 1960). Easy-to-read text and a naughty beast have made this book a winner for many years.

Mother Goose. These wonderful tales have been done up beautifully by both Brian Wildsmith and Raymond Briggs. A Canadian version is *Sharon, Lois and Bram's Mother Goose* (Douglas and McIntyre, 1985) with illustrations by Maryann Kovalski.

Stuff to Encourage Reading

Reading is more than books. Make sure your preschooler has some of the following:

- magnetic fridge letters
- felt board and letters
- easel, pad, and markers
- alphabet placemat
- blackboard

Don't forget the gimmick books: pop-ups, cut-outs, paste-ins, colouring books. They're fun for tiny hands and can help develop both language and a sense of story.

Once that first step is taken, *then* you can include a little informal teaching. Generally speaking, I think inadvertent phonics is far more valuable for young children than formal phonics instruction. Your child doesn't have to master the 200 or so phonics bits to be a good reader, but she might find it helpful for you to break up the occasional word into syllables. She might find it useful, when playing with magnetic letters on the refrigerator, to hear you blend the sounds in a word: "Fi-ish. The *F* makes a 'fi' sound, the *I* sounds like 'ih' and *SH* is 'sh.' Fish." Nothing could be more deadly for a young child than formal, systematic phonics. But every child will find some phonics clues a helpful tool in attacking words she can't pick up at a glance.

What's essential in building your child's reading is your involvement. Early reading is always social. No three-year-old, or five-year-old for that matter, wants to read to herself. Her reading, when it comes, will be out loud – just as your reading, with her, was out loud through the years of early childhood. You have to be there to hear the reading when it happens.

These days, many books for young children are available on audio tape and can be popped into a child's Fisher-Price tape recorder. There's nothing wrong with your child's doing this after you've read the book a few times. Just remember that no tape recorder or videotape can ever substitute for you, your time, and your love.

Reading Together – and Variations

The reading demands of a three- or four-year-old can be quite substantial. While a younger child will frequently be satisfied with a book or two at various times of the day, a three-year-old who says, "Daddy, read to me," will often be prepared to sit for an hour or more and read twenty or thirty books. This kind of marathon might be far more than Daddy had in mind.

So mix it up. Reading a book is only one kind of reading activity. Why not try a few others?

- Draw a picture and make up a story about it.

- Make up a story with your child as the central character.

- Read the newspaper together, especially the comics or children's page.

- Play with letters on the fridge or your child's blackboard.

- Read a magazine like *Chickadee*.

- Write a letter to Grandma, or the Easter bunny, or the Lego News.

- Look through a catalogue or photo album together.

- Tell a story about your own life as a child.

Reading, listening, and language skills all develop together. The more your child reads and hears, the more sophisticated her talking and imagining will become. The great advantage of reading, of course, is that she'll have a chance to hear words that don't come up in ordinary conversation. We have more than 500,000 words in the English language, yet rarely use more than 15,000 in everyday speech. One researcher videotaped three hours of television and found that only 7,000 different words were used in all that time. Neither talk nor television, then, is sufficient to build your child's vocabulary.

Reading, on the other hand, opens a door to language for your child that would otherwise remain closed. It allows her to hear longer sentences, more carefully structured and beautifully balanced than those of everyday speech.

What's more, reading creates windows on parts of the world and experiences that your child will otherwise never get to know. When my children

Some of Canada's Top Author/ Illustrators for Preschoolers

Worldwide recognition has been won by a talented group of Canadian writer/artists. Their books are always worth looking for:

- Barbara Reid lives in Toronto but is known throughout the world for her unique Plasticine illustrations. She's won many awards including the 1987 Ezra Jack Keats award for *Have You Seen Birds?*

- Marie-Louise Gay, the Montreal author/ illustrator, does detailed, sensitive illustrations for young readers. Her book *Rainy Day Magic* won the Governor General's Award in 1988.

- Phoebe Gilman worked at the Ontario College of Art when she began writing children's books with *Balloon Tree* in 1984 and the first Jillian Jiggs book in 1985. Now she writes and illustrates full time in Toronto.

- Maryann Kovalski has illustrated for Allen Morgan, but also writes and illustrates her own books, like *Wheels on the Bus*. Her work is published in Canada, Britain, and the United States.

were young, they loved *Babar and the Moustache Man*. They'd never been to Paris or Africa, never seen a subway, or held a flute, or seen a king. But thanks to the Laurent De Brunhoff classic, all these became part of their early lives.

Books expand language and experience in ways that are obvious, like my Babar example, and ways that are subtle. When your child reads *Franklin in the Dark* by Paulette Bourgeois, she won't learn much about turtles, but she'll find her own fear of the dark validated by seeing it in print. The human-looking animals in picture books are there for a reason: often it's more comforting to recognize our fears in those of a frightened turtle than it is to admit them out loud. Books not only expand the outer world for your child, they articulate the feelings of her inner world as well.

Your Child's Bookshelf – and Still More Books

By the time your child is five, her bookshelf will probably have twenty or thirty books on it. Some you'll have bought, some will be gifts, some you'll get as hand-me-downs, or by trading with other parents. These books are vitally important – but your child will still want to look at and read many more. That's where the public library can help.

If you read for just twenty minutes a day, you and your young child will go through over 100 books each month. Some of these will be favourite books, read over and over again, but many will be on loan from the local library. Your library will likely have most of the titles recommended in this book and thousands of others as well: story-books, fairy-tales, non-fiction books, animal books, books with audio tapes, joke books, photo-illustrated books, poetry books, books about love, death and anger, books about babies and going to school and divorce, books about . . . Well, you get the idea.

When our children were young, my wife and I used the library to bring in a dozen new children's books every week; then we ordered from a bookstore the titles that caught the boys' interest. Since a big illustrated book can cost twenty dollars, the "library-first, bookstore-second" approach gave us a chance to buy books that were sure favourites, because we'd already tested out their appeal when they were on loan from the library. What's more, the selection of children's books in most libraries is much wider than that of even the best bookstore. With 4,500 new children's books published every year, few bookstores can stock even a fraction of what's current. And backlist titles – books that came out last year or the year before – can disappear far too quickly from bookstore shelves. Your library will still have these books and many other titles from a collection that might stretch back over decades. Your child can enjoy them all.

Reading is Special

When reading together, most parents like to hold young children on their laps. Even Alex, my squirmiest son, would sit reasonably still on my lap when he was being read to. Grandparents and baby-sitters may prefer to have children sit beside them, but snuggling close. Some parents read to their children in bed. My own father had a special reading chair, wide enough for my brother and me to sit together on his lap. At day care centres, reading often takes place in small groups, with kids sitting on mats or pillows. The physical arrangements for reading are relatively unimportant. What matters is that there is time for reading.

A few parents like to read in the morning, but this is becoming more difficult for busy, two-income families. My favourite reading time is after school, when I'm relaxed but still have some energy. My parents liked to read right after supper, because they were too sleepy at bedtime. But the favourite reading time of all, of course, is just before bed.

What about *Sesame Street*?

Chances are your young child will end up watching *Sesame Street* once or twice a day. For almost thirty years, the program has been a major part of early childhood, praised for raising the letter- and word-recognition skills of kindergarten kids, condemned for packaging everything into spots as short as ten seconds.

Yet *Sesame Street* does help young children start reading – and so do the Sesame Street books, published inexpensively by Golden Books. These inexpensive spin-off books use characters like Big Bird and Grover from the series. The quality of the books varies enormously, but all have an automatic appeal since your child will have seen the characters on television. My favourites: *Big Bird's Big and Little Book* and *The Monster at the End of This Book*.

Very Early Readers

A certain portion of children start reading well before kindergarten. Two researchers at the University of Saskatchewan sampled 1,400 kindergartners and found twenty very early readers (about 1.5 percent of their population). Other researchers have found that most very early readers don't differ in general intelligence from other children, but they all come from home environments that support reading.

Make sure that reading time is a special time. Older children might be able to read with the TV on, or with headphones blasting rock music into their ears, but young children cannot. Reading time should be a quiet time, a settling time. The TV goes off, your voice begins the story, and the dream begins.

Reading doesn't happen "out there," like the experience of television; the experience of reading is inside us. When your child hears you read *Goodnight Moon* by Margaret Wise Brown, she *becomes* the little rabbit of the story. The wonderful thing about reading is that we enter into the action – we are *in* the book. Reading should always be active and involving.

Never force a book, or keep reading if your child wants to stop. There is a difference between waiting for your child to settle down and dealing with a child who just isn't interested. Don't expect a quiet reading time to be successful right after a boisterous birthday party, or when your child is cranky and tired. Let it go. Don't try to force Dr. Dolittle stories if your child doesn't want to listen to them. On some days, your child won't want to hear even favourite books. That's when you should both take a day off from your daily reading.

Sometimes you'll have to wait until your child is ready for certain books. My youngest child wasn't at all interested in Rupert the Bear books when he was four and at home, but he found great delight in them at the cottage when he was eight. The book that bores one day may well amuse the next day, or next week, or next year. In reading, as in so much else, parents must be patient.

Relax and enjoy. Young children are responsive and curious and loving when you read with them. Their books will be a joy to both you and your child. Soon enough your child will be too large to sit on your lap any more. Make sure you have many days and many books to remember before she's off in her own chair with a book.

Twelve Must-have Books for Your Very Young Child's Bookshelf

Janet and Allan Ahlberg, *Each Peach Pear Plum* (Scholastic, 1978). Really a peekaboo game in a book – great for reading together with your kids.

Margaret Wise Brown, *Goodnight Moon* (Harper-Collins, 1947). Simple and repetitive for adults but the best bedtime book ever for young children.

Paulette Bourgeois, *Franklin in the Dark* (Kids Can, 1986). Illustrations by Brenda Clark. The charming story of Franklin, the timid turtle, who overcomes his fear of the dark. First of the Franklin series by one of Canada's top children's authors.

P.D. Eastman, *Are You My Mother?* (Random House, 1960). A young bird falls from his nest and has to find his mother. Warm and charming.

Ezra Jack Keats, *The Snowy Day* (Puffin, 1962). A boy makes a snowball and keeps it in his pocket. Street-smart illustrations by an American award-winner.

Maryann Kovalski, *The Wheels on the Bus* (Kids-Can, 1987). A fun book, especially if you can sing the song.

Robert Kraus, *Whose Mouse Are You?* (Collier Macmillan, 1970). Identity and family are the themes in one of the most beautiful and moving children's books ever written.

Leo Lionni, *Frederick* (Pantheon, 1966). A wonderful story about a poet/mouse who saves up warm words for winter.

Mercer Mayer, *A Boy, a Dog and a Frog* (Dial, 1967). No words, but evocative drawings to tell the story and to discuss with your child.

Robert Munsch, *Thomas' Snowsuit* (Annick, 1985). Because it really is hard to get dressed to go out and play. A good starter book from Canada's most prolific children's writer.

Richard Scarry, *The Best Word Book Ever* (Golden, 1963). Scarry's books are detailed encyclopaedias for the young, and always well done.

Maurice Sendak, *Where the Wild Things Are* (HarperCollins, 1963). Beautiful, quirky and adventurous. Scary for some young readers, but worth it.

Dr. Seuss, *The Cat in the Hat* (Random House, 1957). A brilliant phonics lesson in a very clever package, now a cultural icon.

CHAPTER 5

The Beginning Reader: Ages Five to Eight

The big new factor in your child's life at age five is school, serious school. Many very young children now attend nursery school and junior kindergartens where good programs put an emphasis on enriching your child's experience with creative play and lots of time spent reading books. But full kindergarten and the primary grades one, two, and three are different: here, your child is expected to learn in a more structured way.

Your child's teachers in these first four years will attempt to teach a great variety of skills – from reading and math to shoelace-tying – to a great variety of children. The goals in reading are to have every child master the basics by the end of grade three. These basics include recognition of the alphabet, a quick sight vocabulary of 3,000 or more everyday words, enough phonics to tackle more difficult words, and a comfortable reading speed so stories can be read silently and with some enjoyment.

Schools try to do all this with one teacher in a classroom of twenty-five kids with an enormous range of abilities and backgrounds. That real learning takes place in such circumstances is a tribute to the natural curiosity of children and to the wonderful dedication of primary teachers.

With luck, your child will be with a good teacher in a good school. Then you're likely to see some of the following:

- parent volunteers to help with reading, field trips, special activities, and the library;

- peer tutors – grade seven and eight students working with younger children in reading and mathematics;

- a strong library program, with check-out privileges starting in kindergarten and the librarian who acts as a reading teacher and enthusiast;

- group learning with kids clustered in different groups – sometimes based on ability, or interest, or friendship – for a variety of learning tasks;

- labels on almost everything in class, colourful bulletin boards, pictures of the kids, awards for virtually any achievement;

- and books – not just primers, but real books, worn out from reading and rereading.

If you don't see much of this, then reread Chapter 3 and put pressure on your school and school board. And do it directly – not by complaining in front of your child. He'll pick up the attitude that his school and teacher are lousy, and that won't help any of you to improve the situation. For school to do its job, your child must see that formal education is important in your eyes. Ms. Jones might not be the world's best teacher, but she is the best teacher your child will ever have for grade one. Be enthusiastic. Ask questions about what happens in school. Phone or drop notes to the teacher about absences or problems at home that she should know about. Become a partner in your child's education, even if there's work to do in making it better.

Learning To Read in School

In the past, learning to read at home was fun and learning to read at school was formal. At home, kids would read books; at school, they'd read basal readers or primers. At home, kids would sit on your lap and ask questions as you read; at school, they'd sit in desks and sound out bunches of *B* words. At home, kids would learn to read and love reading; at school, alas, the results were spotty.

Thank goodness, things have changed. These days, good schools try to simulate the home reading environment as much as possible. The old phonics drills have disappeared; the Dick and Jane readers have become real books; the desk work has been replaced by a cosy reading corner. Instead of phonics and colour-the-mimeo-graphed-page, we have "children's literature" and "big books" that are printed on huge pages and can be seen at the back of the classroom. This whole language approach seems to be producing the most literate group of young people in history – up to grade four.

You shouldn't be upset that the schools aren't drilling your child with phonics. There is no real evidence that formal instruction in phonics rules produces more readers than any other technique. For some children – perhaps that quarter of the student population who can apply theoretical rules to real situations – formal phonics is an effective means of learning to read. For most others, phonics is just one more tool for figuring out what the tough words are.

The current approach in schools recognizes that different children learn in different ways (the buzz phrase is "learning styles"). For some children, reading just clicks without formal instruction. For others, phonics is essential for

School Books Clubs and Fairs

Once your child begins attending school, he'll sometimes have a chance to buy books at special school book fairs. These are book sales, often organized by the school librarian and held in the gym or cafeteria, where a local bookstore or book wholesaler offers a wide range of books to kids and sometimes to their parents. If your child's school doesn't have such an event, it's worth suggesting.

The most popular school book clubs in Canada are run by Scholastic Publishing (123 Newkirk Road, Richmond Hill, Ontario L4C 3G5). The clubs offer a selection of titles every month, mostly published by Scholastic but from other publishers as well. The club name depends on your child's age: Elf for preschoolers; See-Saw for kindergarten and grade one; Lucky for grades two and three; Arrow for grades four, five, and six; Tab for grades seven, eight and nine.

making sense of words on the printed page. For still others, context clues or word games work better. The style with which your child learns best will help determine what kind of teaching will be most effective for him.

The whole language approach in schools tries to accommodate many different styles of learning – and preserve some of the sheer joy in reading. Chances are your child will read – and have read to him – many more books than you did in the primary grades. Chances are your child will master about as many phonic rules as you did, though not in such a rigorous way. And chances are your child will enjoy reading in school much more than those kids at the back of the class did thirty years ago.

Reading at Home

Regardless of how good your child's school may be, the most important reading environment is not the classroom or the school library. The single most important reading environment is your home.

- Continue to read every day with your child. No matter how independent he may appear, he still needs your interest and your time. If your home is going through a period of stress, this quiet time together with you will be even more important. Many young children suffer through the turmoil of divorce or a parent's job insecurity. Mom and Dad may be fighting, or too preoccupied to pay attention to the kids. Children can't articulate their needs for love and care, but they do show family stress through restlessness, attention-seeking behaviour in school, and limited concentration span. Sometimes parents need to examine their home life seriously so their children can get the stability they need to grow. Daily

Governor General's "Illustrations" Award Winners

The top Canadian prize for writers and illustrators is the GG (renamed from the Canada Council Children's Literature Prize in 1987). Here are the winners in English:

1991: Joanne Fitzgerald, *Dr. Kiss Says Yes* (Groundwood, 1991). Text by Teddy Jam.
1990: Paul Morin, *The Orphan Boy* (Oxford, 1989). Text by Tololwa Mollel.
1989: Robin Muller, *The Magic Paintbrush* (Doubleday, 1989).
1988: Kim LeFave, *Amos' Sweater* (Groundwood, 1988). Text by Janet Lunn.
1987: Marie-Louise Gay, *Rainy Day Magic* (Stoddart, 1987).
1986: Barbara Reid, *Have You Seen Birds?* (Scholastic, 1986). Text by Joan Oppenheim.
1985: Terry Gallagher, *Murdo's Story* (Pemmican, 1986). Text by Murdo Scribe.
1984: Marie-Louise Gay, *Lizzy's Lion* (Stoddart, 1984). Text by Dennis Lee.
1983: Laszlo Gal, *The Little Mermaid* (Methuen, 1983). Text by Margaret Maloney Crawford.
1982: Vlasta van Kampen, *ABC, 123* (Hurtig, 1982).
1981: Heather Woodall, *Ytek and the Arctic Orchid* (Douglas & McIntyre, 1981).

reading time, whatever else might be going on, can be an important island of security for your child.

- Continue to reach into your wallet to buy many kinds of print material. Your child learns about the variety of what he can read by seeing books, magazines, newsletters, cookbooks, newspapers, family letters, clippings, postcards, cereal-box backs and anything else with print on it lying around the house. Your child learns about the value of reading by watching you read. He must see that reading is important to you for reading to become important for him.

- Continue to make sure that your child has time to read at home. Quiet time. Time with the TV turned off. Time with you. Your child's school will devote an hour a day to reading for the 180 days of the school year. You can double that time simply by reading with your child for half an hour each day right through the calendar year.

A good time to review rules on watching television is when your child is entering school. Since school will be taking up six to eight hours a day, less time is available to do everything else. To keep some balance in your child's life, explain, that the television has to be kept under control. The research doesn't say that you should throw the TV away, or limit it to an hour a day – the research says, set rules. I suspect every family already has rules on television viewing which they never even think about: turn it off at midnight, keep it quiet before the parents get up, no TV at dinner. All I'm suggesting is that these rules be extended so there is some structure in your child's free time and enough quiet time for reading to happen.

Parent-to-Parent
Problems Also Start at Home

"In the late 1960s, I had to examine honestly how our home life was affecting our three children. My son Robert had failed kindergarten twice. Yes, twice! The reason for Robert's problems was not too much TV or any learning disability. It was the explosive situation in which he lived, caused by our unhappy marriage.

"After I left with all three children, Robert progressed rapidly and was working at an average grade three level by the time he was in third grade. Things continued to improve. Today he has two degrees and works as a systems analyst for the Royal Bank in Toronto. I think his progress has a lot to do with the fact that I was honest enough to see what was wrong with my child's home situation.

"A home where parents fight or argue isn't conducive for a child learning to read. In Canada, where almost half our marriages end in divorce, many children face unhappy social situations in their own homes. A child can't read if he is fearful, apprehensive, or uncertain about what will happen next."

– (name withheld)

These early school years are crucial to teach decision-making and self-reliance. A child who has to make up his mind just which two or three hours of television to watch is also making decisions about what to do with the other hours in the day. When you say, "Two hours of TV a day is enough," you're also saying, "Now decide what you want to do with the other three hours before bed." By making yourself available to help, reading will be one of those choices.

Building the Bookshelf

By now, your child should have more than a dozen favourite books on his bookshelf. These books haven't become obsolete just because your child is beginning to read for himself. But now he needs new and different books, with an emphasis on those he'll be able to read for himself. Although Ian Wallace's *Chin Chiang and the Dragon's Dance* is a beautiful book, it requires reading skills that are too sophisticated for beginning readers. Paulette Bourgeois' *Big Sarah's Little Boots* is more closely linked to reading skills at the grade one/two level. By reading daily with your child, you'll know just how good your child's reading skills are.

If your child is choosing his own books, he'll naturally pick books written at a level he can read. If you're doing the choosing, look for the qualities that make a book easy for beginning readers to read:

- simple vocabulary and short sentences – because beginner's recognition vocabularies are small and their reading speed is slow;

- not too much print on a page – because it's frustrating for any reader to be stuck too long on one page;

- illustrations to give clues about the story – even if a picture isn't worth a thousand

The Caldecott Award Winners

These prestigious awards go back to 1938. They recognize the "best" American illustrated book for young children in any given year. Here are the most recent winners:

1991: David Macaulay, *Black and White* (Houghton Mifflin, 1990).

1990: Ed Young, *Lon Po Po: A Red Riding Hood Story from China* (Philomel, 1989).

1989: Karen Ackerman, *Song and Dance Man* (Knopf, 1988).

1988: Jane Yolen, *Owl Moon* (Philomel, 1987).

1987: Arthur Yorinks, *Hey Al* (Farrar, Strauss, 1986).

1986: Chris Van Allsburg, *Polar Express* (Houghton Mifflin, 1985).

1985: Margaret Hodges, *Saint George and the Dragon* (Little, Brown, 1984).

1984: Alice Provensen, *Glorious Flight* (Puffin, 1983).

1983: Blaise Cendrars, *Shadow* (Scribners, 1982).

1982: Chris Van Allsburg, *Jumanji* (Houghton Mifflin, 1981).

1981: Arnold Lobel, *Fables* (Harper-Collins, 1980).

1980: Donald Hall, *Ox Cart Man* (Puffin, 1979).

words, it might give clues about one or
two tough ones;

- relatively large type – because it's easier
to read;

- a "predictable" text, but not so predictable it becomes boring to you or your child.
A book doesn't have to sound like Dick
and Jane to be easy to read.

When your child begins to read for himself, a
number of things will happen all at once. The
first is usually memorization. Your child will
have read one favourite book over and over
again until the words are memorized. Then,
magically, your child will begin to connect those
words to the print on the accompanying page.
This mixture of recognition and remembering is
often the first reading. That's the reason children
can "read" favourite books with vocabulary ranging from *Alexander* to *zoological* even though
those words are much more sophisticated than
they could possibly recognize or sound out.

Other children will begin reading with simple
words they can recognize at a glance. The single-
syllable vocabulary of P.D. Eastman's *Go, Dog,
Go* includes the short, commonplace words that
are easiest for young children to recognize without help. You'll find other books with the same
approach. If your child likes to pick out words he
can recognize, then these are the books you
should be reading again and again.

Some children will combine words they know
with phonics rules to sound out others. This
process is painfully slow at first, but it can
handle the more difficult vocabulary in books
like Judith Viorst's *Alexander and the Terrible,
Horrible, No Good, Very Bad Day*. If your child
takes well to phonics, your choice of books is
very wide. But you must be there to help in
sounding out. Unlike German or Italian, in which
words almost always "sound-out" quite readily,
English is quite erratic. Your child will need help

The Five-Finger Reading Check

When your child starts to read for himself,
it's important that the books he tackles
aren't too difficult for him to handle successfully. Teachers have a simple way to
match kids with the reading difficulty of a
book: the five-finger check.

Ask your child to read a page from a
book. Everytime he stumbles or skips a
word, curl up one of your fingers. If all five
fingers are curled up by the end of the
page, the book is too tough. Read it to him
this time, and put off his own reading for
later on.

sounding out and blending sounds to make sure *Ottawa* doesn't come out "Ah-tah'-wa," and sound like a city in Japan. We all read in order to pull meaning from the printed page. The danger in phonics is that even careful reading will produce nonsense. This is the time a parent must help.

The key to all beginner books is a certain predictability in the text. Books for both younger and older children can offer prose rich in poetic language and surprising turns of phrase. For younger children, this richness works because you are doing the reading; for older children, it works because they have the skills to read more difficult material. But the first books your child reads for himself should be predictable: a regular rhythm, a repeated sentence structure, or a repeated set of lines (like a refrain in poetry) to make easier the task of looking at words or sounding out what's on the page. Dr. Seuss books have been starting young readers off for more than thirty years because the author understood just what young children need to read on their own.

Keep It Fun

Beginning reading shouldn't be work – it should be fun. Your child has lots of time to learn to decode words on a page – and this is only one stage in that whole process. So don't load on the pressure. Many children at A.S. Neill's Summerhill school in England didn't learn to read until they were teenagers, but within a year or so they were able to catch up with their more traditionally educated peers. There is no magic timetable for learning how to read. There are no particular skills or drills that will make it happen. And nothing will turn your child off reading more than too much pressure from you. All you have to do is enjoy reading to your child. Sooner or later, your child will take over the reading from you.

In the last chapter, we looked at reading to a

Some of Canada's Top Author/ Illustrators for Older Readers

- Robin Muller is known for his dark, magical, and often scary illustrations in books like *The Magic Paintbrush* and *Nightwood* (Doubleday 1989, 1991). His original art is held in many collections from Rothman's to CITY-TV.

- Steve Pilcher is the young artist of the *Norbert Nipkin* series (Napoleon, 1989, etc.). His highly exaggerated and striking drawings are either loved or hated by adult readers.

- Stephane Poulin has won Canada Council awards for two of his books, including *Can You Catch Josephine* (Tundra, 1988). His sense of whimsy shows in the subtitle to *Travels for Two: Stories and Lies from My Childhood*.

- Ian Wallace studied at the Ontario College of Art and began illustrating children's books with *Chin Chiang and the Dragon's Dance* (Groundwood). His illustrations of his own stories and those by other writers have been recognized around the world.

three-year-old. When Marcia Baghban read to young Gita, the emphasis was on the baby's responses, on participation, on remembering key words. There was no "reading" in the sense of decoding print on the page, but there was lots of real reading going on.

Now let's listen to Janie Jardine of Collingwood, Ontario, read with her seven-year-old son, John. The story is Roch Carrier's *The Hockey Sweater*, one which is still too difficult for John to read on his own.

MOM: (reading) *The winters of my childhood were long, long seasons. We lived in three places* – see in the picture –

JOHN: Yeah, it's snowing, like outside.

MOM: That's true. (reading) – *the church, the school and the skating rink. But our real life was on the skating rink* –

John nods. (He's a hockey player himself.)

MOM: (reading) *Real battles were won on the skating rink. Real strength appeared on the skating rink. The real leaders showed themselves on the skating rink. School was sort of a punishment. Parents always want to punish their children and school is their most natural way of punishing them.*

John shakes his head.

MOM: You don't think so?

JOHN: School's okay.

MOM: Well, maybe when this book was written schools weren't so much fun. (reads) *However, school was also a quiet place where we could prepare for the next hockey game and lay out our next strategy. As for church, we found there the tranquillity of God. There we forgot school and* dreamed *about our next hockey game.*

Psst . . . Don't Tell the Kids, These Books Are Really for Us

Here are some books that your kids will love, but you'll enjoy even more:

Roy Gerrard, *Sir Cedric Rides Again* (Gollancz, 1984). A balding knight in a rhyming tale of derring-do.

Alexander Wolf and Jon Scieszka, *The True Story of the Three Little Pigs* (Viking, 1989). Told from the innocent wolf's point-of-view, of course.

James Marshall, *George and Martha* (Houghton, Mifflin, 1972). Charming and insightful stories about the ongoing lives of two hippopotamuses. Good for your relationship and your funny bone.

Robert Munsch, *The Paper Bag Princess* (Annick, 1990). This book started the whole Munsch phenomenon. A sprightly princess gives a politically correct twist to an otherwise straight fairy-tale.

Shel Silverstein, *Where the Sidewalk Ends* (HarperCollins, 1974). Wild line drawings combine with Silverstein's sardonic, neurotic humour.

John smiles.

MOM: (reading) *Through our daydreams it might happen that we would recite a prayer and ask God to help us play as well as Maurice Richard* – Do you know who Maurice Richard is?

JOHN: No.

MOM: He was a famous hockey player when I was a young girl. He was born in, uh, 1925.

JOHN: Is he still alive?

MOM: I don't know. I think he is.

JOHN: Okay, read some more.

This transcript shows you exactly why your involvement with reading is so important. Not only are John's reading skills too limited to handle words like *tranquillity,* his experience is too limited to understand just why Maurice Richard and the Montreal Canadiens should be so important to the young boy in the story. His mother can fill in these gaps and help relate the story to John's life. What's more, her reading is expanding John's universe. John is listening to a story, but he's also learning vocabulary, a bit of history, and a sense of what life was like in Quebec in the 1940s.

Much of the time you and your child spend reading together will still involve *you* as the reader – even though your child can read for himself. But with easy and familiar books, your child might be more than willing to help out with some of the reading. Here's a transcript of an old family tape of me reading, from Dr. Seuss' *Green Eggs and Ham* with my son Alex who was then six years old. Alex was reading some of the pages, I was reading the others.

DAD: Can you read the sign?

ALEX: *I am Sam.* (page turn) Zoom. *I am*

Sam. (page turn) *Sam I am!*

DAD: *That Sam-I-am! That Sam-I-am! I do not like that –*

ALEX: *Sam I am.* (page turn) (To Dad) No, me. (reading) *Do you like green eggs and ham?*

DAD: *I do not like them, Sam-I-am.*

ALEX (shouting) and Dad: *I do not like green eggs and ham.*

Was Alex reading or was he reciting memorized passages? I don't think it really matters. What's important is that the experience of reading is shared and it's fun.

Don't spend a lot of time correcting your child if he makes a mistake, or prodding him into reading himself if he doesn't want to. All that will fix itself over time. But you can make deals that will help the process. My middle son was a very good reader early on, but a very lazy one. He'd far rather have Dad read to him than read himself, so I ended up bargaining with him. I'd start a story, read about half, and then say, "Oh, I'm getting tired now, Justin. I think we'll have to finish it tomorrow." He'd complain, so I'd reply, "Well, my voice is tired so why don't you read a few pages and give me a rest, then I'll finish up." It worked – almost every time.

Our goal as parents is to build our child's skills so he will be able to read when we're not around. We start by reading all the words, then gradually encourage our child to read more and more on his own. With my boys, by age seven, I was simply the guy who held them on his lap and turned the pages. Ironically, when my children were older and had become very accomplished readers, I went back to my first role. I was the one who did virtually all the reading out loud. Then they'd carry on themselves, silently, long after I left the bedroom.

Five Reading Games

Easy games for beginning readers – not to replace reading out loud, but to offer some variety.

Trade a page. "I'll read one page and you read one page. Deal?" This is the opening gambit for rereading a favourite book. Of course, you'll help your son when he gets stuck on a word, and sometimes you'll end up reading more than one page. But by doing half the reading at a regular pace, you'll keep the meaning of the book clear.

Hot Dog. "Hot Dog" is the word you throw in every so often: "The three little pigs lived in a hot dog in the forest." The quick response: "No, Mommy. House!" A fun game that will also keep your child's eyes following the print.

Fill the blank. Read along normally right up to the end of the page, then stop with three words to go. "How about you finish up? You can read the words."

Change the hero's name. Who says that *Thomas' Snowsuit* has to be about Thomas if your son is named Julian? Who says that the hero of a boy's book can't be a girl named Jill? Bring your child into the story.

Funny sounds, funny voices. Many children's books have places for exaggerated sound effects written in. "Bzzzz went the saw" and jiggle your child. Or try doing one character's voice with a Spanish accent or in a falsetto.

Many Different Books for the Beginning Reader

Your beginning reader will probably enjoy many of the same children's books that you do. But if you'd like to tune in more directly to the special interests of the age-five-to-eight crowd, here are some suggestions:

- Humour always works. Try the Berenstains' *Inside, Outside, Upside Down,* or some simple joke books, or the poems in Dennis Lee's new book *The Ice Cream Store.*

- Animals. Kids have a fondness for animals, both real and imaginary. They even like to read about dinosaurs, though there haven't been any around for sixty-five million years. Books like Arnold Lobel's *Frog and Toad All Year* and William Steig's beautifully illustrated *The Amazing Bone* tie into these interests.

- The real life of kids. Judith Viorst's *Alexander and the Terrible, Horrible, No Good, Very Bad Day* has quickly become a classic. Bob Munsch's *Thomas' Snowsuit* and *I Have to Go* are delightfully honest about the trials and tribulations of a young child's life.

- Poetry and rhyme. Nothing's more fun than a book you can chant or sing. Try sean o'huigan's *Scary Poems for Rotten Kids* or Sonja Dunn's chants as well as the Dennis Lee books.

- Your child's interests. If your son is playing T-ball, get a baseball book like Martyn Godfrey's *Baseball Crazy* and read it together. If your daughter is wild about horses, try Walter Farley's *The Black Stallion.* Neither of these books is easy for young kids to read for themselves, but your child's fascination with the subject will make up the difference.

- TV tie-ins. Nothing's wrong with Sesame Street books – they're never inspired, but always good enough. The same can be said for Disney books or even books that are spin-off products from a currently popular movie. No child was ever hurt by reading schlock – so long as it's not the entire literary diet.

Beginning readers – and their parents – have an amazing appetite for books. You'll go through hundreds in the space of three years: good books, lousy ones, beautiful books, plain ones, favourite books, and one-read-only books, books you'll both love and books that will make you groan.

Your child will choose books just as adults do – by the cover, by the obvious content, by what a page looks like. Sometimes their choices will become repetitive. After all, just how many Teenage Mutant Ninja Turtles books are you prepared to read to your six-year-old? And some very valuable books – books with history or moral lessons or important ideas – won't jump off the library shelves into your child's hands. Use some parental discretion. "Sure, I'll read *Clifford the Dog* again, but then I want to try this book of African folk-tales." Ultimately, we can never force our children to enjoy a book, but we can make some effort to broaden their tastes.

I've always thought that the magic of these early books – for both parent and child – could never quite be matched by what my children read later on. Let me suggest that you use audio or video tape to record one of the reading sessions with your young child. The memories will touch your heart later on and bring back what was a very fine time, indeed.

Four Magazines for Beginning Readers

- *Electric Company.* From the creators of the television show: colourful, playful, and slick.

- *Chickadee and Owl.* Two award-winning, profusely illustrated magazines which just happen to be Canadian. Both focus on the environment with lots of hands-on activities. *Chickadee* works best at grades one and two; *Owl* in grades three and four.

- *Ranger Rick* from the National Wildlife Foundation. Very short articles on animals but great illustrations for projects.

- *Stone Soup.* A literary magazine for kids with a great deal of art work for young Rembrandts.

Twelve Must-have, Easy-to-read Books for Your Child's Bookshelf

Norman Bridwell, *Clifford Takes a Trip* (Scholastic, 1985). Take one large, amusing dog and some big print and you have a very popular easy-to-read book.

The Berenstains, *Inside, Outside, Upside Down* (Random House, 1968) and many other titles. Adorable bears and simple text make all these books winners.

Paulette Bourgeois, *Big Sarah's Little Boots* (KidsCan, 1987). Sarah has outgrown her boots and she's frustrated about growing up. Simple vocabulary and good, easy-to-read style.

P.D. Eastman, *Go, Dog, Go* (Random House, 1965). Simple vocabulary but an endearing story. A good "favourite book" because the text is short and predictable.

Phoebe Gilman, *The Wonderful Pigs of Jillian Jiggs* (Scholastic, 1988). A beautiful book about love and sharing. It rhymes and comes with an activity section so you can make your own pigs.

Dennis Lee, *Alligator Pie* (Macmillan, 1984). The most famous book by Canada's famed children's poet; it may still be his best. Witty, gutsy, appealing poetry that will stick in your child's memory.

A.A. Milne, *Winnie-the-Pooh*. A 1926 classic that comes in many versions. You'll have to help with reading the original, but many of the Disney-ized Golden Books are easy enough for your child to read on his own.

Robert Munsch. With thirty books in print, from tiny Annikins to full-sized hardcovers, Munsch is a veritable industry in Canada. Any title will be just fine, but my favourite is still *The Paper Bag Princess* (Annick, 1980).

Gordon Penrose, *Dr. Zed's Science Surprises* (Greey de Pencier, 1988). This book is full of fun for you and your child and shows that reading offers more than just stories.

Dr. Seuss, *One Fish, Two Fish* (Random House, 1960) and many other titles. Among the first and still the best of beginner-book authors.

Marcia Vaugh, *Goldsworthy and Mort* (Harper-Collins, 1991). Two animal friends in adventures like *Wind In the Willows,* but your child can read this book himself.

Judith Viorst, *Alexander and the Terrible, Horrible, No Good, Very Bad Day* (Maxwell Macmillan, 1972). The title says it all. You'll have to read the text for the first few times, then the book's rhythm and repetition will let your child take over.

CHAPTER 6

The Middle Reader: Ages Eight to Ten

Jennifer is in grade four. She reads for herself now, sometimes picture books from earlier years, sometimes short novels that she brings home from the school library. She reads silently with good speed and understanding. She reads out loud with expression and only a few problems with difficult words. She enjoys your reading to her, and frequently takes over when you say you're tired. Sometimes you feel that your job is finished – that Jennifer is all set up to be a reader for life.

But it's not that easy.

Your child has only begun to build her skills in reading, and she still has a great many more to learn. She enjoys books now, but if enough distractions occur she might well turn away from books. Grade four is the year in which as many as a third of our children stop bothering to read. Dr. Jeanne Chall of Harvard University calls this the "fourth grade slump," a problem that seems to affect boys more than girls, but which can afflict any child.

For the child who gets caught in fourth grade slump, the time spent reading declines rapidly, concentration decreases, and vocabulary growth slows down. The child's reading development becomes stalled right after it's begun, like a plane whose engines cut out just as it's taking off.

This is a tragedy, but it can be prevented by parents who are still involved in their children's reading. The solution is to continue with the basics: reading out loud with your child, buying at least one new book a month, and keeping rules on television watching and other distractions.

So long as you continue with the basics, you need not panic if you see signs of a slump in reading interest. To some extent, slumps and setbacks are natural as part of any child's mental growth. Researchers suspect that before each stage of intellectual development, a child has to consolidate what she has already learned. Before moving on to first novels, a child might limit herself to familiar picture books for a period of months. Before taking over the daily reading almost entirely, she may insist that Mom read *everything*. Rather than getting upset or overly worried when your child seems to be regressing, parents have to understand that this stage could be a necessary one before the next big jump can be made. Your child's brain is somehow solidifying what it already knows so she can move on. You've got to support that process when it occurs. Yet you also have to be watchful in case a temporary slump is a sign of a more serious problem. See Chapters 10 and 11 if any setback seems to last for more than a month or two.

Resources: Canadian Children's Book Centre

Located in a renovated mansion on Spadina Road in Toronto, the Canadian Children's Book Centre is this country's top authority on children's books. They

- provide information about any of Canada's children's authors and illustrators;

- produce a number of publications for teachers and an excellent bibliography for parents called *Reading: A Lifelong Adventure*;

- have a library of thousands of Canadian children's books;

- sponsor outreach activities that send authors and illustrators to visit schools around the country.

To contact, write or phone
Canadian Children's Book Centre
35 Spadina Road
Toronto, Ontario M5R 2S9
(416) 975-0010

Daily Reading

By now, your child has probably taken over a fair amount of your daily reading, but that doesn't mean you've stopped being important. By continuing to be part of family reading time, you're providing three important things:

- your presence,
- proper pronunciation and explanations of unfamiliar words,
- improved comprehension.

Your presence validates the importance of reading to your child, and it silently applauds her success. You are also beside her if she gets in trouble – when the sentence doesn't make sense, or she can't pronounce a word, or she doesn't know what a word means.

Some researchers suspect that the difference between children who glide over the grade four slump and those who are stalled by it is simple – vocabulary. The books read in middle school and up require much bigger vocabularies than the basal readers and controlled-vocabulary books of the primary grades. Your child ultimately needs to be familiar with many more than the "magic 3,000" words recognized by the average nine-year-old to read confidently the 120,000 words that a competent adult recognizes. By being with her at reading time, you're there to explain difficult words.

Through your talk about the book or story, you're also assisting in better comprehension of the print. Reading, as I've said, isn't just decoding the words on the page; it's understanding and thinking about the ideas or images behind those words. Your daughter isn't reading just because she can sound out Mordecai Richler's *Jacob Two-Two Meets the Hooded Fang.* She's reading when she can feel Jacob's terror and picture the Hooded Fang in her own mind. Your presence and interest help that to happen.

Let's listen to eight-year-old James Bradshaw reading with his mother, Diana. James is a very bright student who had just finished a Hardy Boys book as part of a school read-a-thon. This transcript records him reading *Star Trek VI: The Undiscovered Country*, which he had bought at a school book fair. The text is somewhat too difficult for him, but with Diana's help he can succeed even with this adult-level novel.

JAMES: *Admiral Cartwright rose angrily, "I must protest. To offer the Klingons a safe haa-ven . . .*

Some Easy Books, Just for Fun

These books are all easy-to-read and fun – for you and your child.

John Bianchi, *The Bungalo Boys* (Bungalo Books, 1986). First of a series of books about a team of bumbling misfits. Good slapstick.

Helen Levchuk and John Bianchi, *The Dingles* (Douglas & McIntyre, 1985). A weird family and their cats. You may enjoy the satire more than your child will.

Allen Morgan, *Matthew and the Midnight Turkeys* (Annick, 1985). Bizarre but cute for younger kids. You'll never look at turkeys the same way again.

sean o'huigin, *Scary Poems for Rotten Kids* (Black Moss, 1982). Poetry much like Dennis Lee's but with an edge to it.

Stephane Poulin, *Can You Catch Josephine?* (Tundra, 1987). Something like *Where's Waldo*, but there's some amusing reading here.

MOM: That's haven. It means a safe place.

JAMES: *A haven within Federation space is . . . suicide. Klingons would become an alien underclass. If we dis– dismantle the fleet, we'd be defenceless before an aggressive species with a . . .* what?

MOM: *Foothold.*

JAMES: Oh, it looks like foo'th'old. (reads) – *foothold on our territory. Led by an unprincipled tyrant?*

Mom nods.

"Boys' " Books and "Girls' " Books

At the turn of the century, boys' books were fully of daring and adventure, while girls' books offered models of mothering and housekeeping. Thank goodness, times have changed.

Nonetheless, boys and girls do tend to read somewhat different books, beginning in middle school, when peer group pressure becomes so important. Most girls remain quite willing to read a book whose central character is a boy, perhaps because they read well enough to project themselves into any character. Boys, alas, become increasingly unwilling to read any book that has a girl as the central character. Maybe the young male sexual identity is that much more fragile.

It will be interesting to see if this pattern holds into the next century.

And the reading went on. James had little difficulty reading even such bizarre words as *Klingons* and *Romulans* because he watches *Star Trek* on TV, but other words like *foothold* gave him some problems. Here, Diana's input was important. She could correct pronunciations as they came up and provide explanations when James needed them. Children, like adults, will frequently skip over short, difficult sections of print to keep the story going. But they'll ask a question when a word or phrase interferes with overall meaning. I doubt that eight-year-old James could define "unprincipled tyrant" but he was sure enough of the meaning in context to go ahead after a quick look at Mom to check pronunciation. If he was really confused by the phrase, Diana was there to offer help.

James struggled through about sixty pages of *Star Trek* before abandoning it. He could have asked Diana to continue reading it out loud to him, but he preferred to go back to reading that he could handle more easily. Middle readers will frequently do this: attempt a difficult adult book, then return to something that really suits them. Sometimes they even reread favourite picture books from early childhood. As a parent, you need to support all this reading – for the challenge, the joy, and the consolidation of reading skills.

Like many middle school children, James is very proud of his reading. He will often tell his parents that he doesn't need their help. This was technically true for his last book, *The Hardy Boys Mystery of the Samurai Sword*, which James read to me for twenty minutes and stumbled over only a single word (jimmied – which needed a definition). But James still needs someone to talk to about swords and scabbards and sword hilts, someone to grab a big picture book on Japan to show him a ceremonial sword, someone to ask just a few questions about how the mystery is developing.

That someone ought to be you. Middle school children will also talk to their friends, brothers, sisters, teachers, grandparents, and the school librarian – but it is your attention that gives reading such value in your child's eyes. A nine-year-old is perfectly capable of reading alone, up in her bedroom or down in the basement. But if reading loses its social context, if it becomes entirely a private experience, then it will lose much of its joy.

Your role in daily reading will already have changed by this time. When you read with your child at age seven, the reading often stopped when you left the room. Now the reading will likely continue for up to an hour after you've left. This practice leads to a certain amount of discontinuity – you end up reading half of chapter 2, and half of chapter 6, and you never do find out how the story ends. But it also gives you a chance to ask your child to fill you in on the story that you've missed.

As your child grows, the function of your reading is much less focused on the mechanics of words and decoding, and much more on discussion of what's happening. By actually reading a page yourself, you'll be able to ask questions whose answers will give you an interesting window on your child's own opinions. Daily reading is as much about your relationship to

The Guest Reader

Throughout this book, I've been talking about the importance of daily reading time. The best reader, of course, is you. But "guest readers" can offer some variety for your child. Older brothers and sisters frequently serve as guest readers in families – and this benefits both them and the younger child. Grandparents are important guest readers for many families, especially if they live in the house or close by.

But guest readers need not be relatives. Family friends can be wonderful readers. If you regularly read to your child before bed, why not ask a dinner guest if he'd mind reading for five minutes while you get dessert ready. The results are often delightful – for your child and your guest. And you'll have plenty to talk about over dessert.

your child as it is about reading. Don't stop just because your child is capable of sitting in her own chair and reading a book to herself.

What Your Child Probably Knows Now

The older children become, the more difficult it is to generalize about what they should or shouldn't know. Every child develops at her own pace. Some children read fluently and avidly at age six, others not until age nine, and I have known some who didn't get excited about reading until twelve or fifteen. For each of these chapters, I've indicated an age span to correspond to a reading stage. But these are guidelines. There are no rules on the speed at which your child will develop.

At the same time, you naturally want your child to keep up with her classmates. You want her to have the reading skills that school will require not just in language arts but also in math, geography, and history. So let me generalize a bit on the basis of what schools expect of students and what research says about children as they go into grades three, four, and five.

- **Phonics**. By the end of grade three, most children know the basic principles of phonics (vowels sounds, consonants, diphthongs like *ay* and *ey*, phonograms like *ight* and *tion*) and can blend phonic pieces together to form words. Teaching of new skills in phonics slows down markedly in grade four and is usually tied to spelling, where phonics is quite helpful, rather than reading, where phonics is only a tool.

- **Sight vocabulary and reading speed**. By the beginning of grade four, most children can quickly recognize most of the words that Jeanne Chall calls the "magic 3,000." Once these 3,000 words can be

Five Scary Books for Middle Schoolers

Sylvia Cassedy, *Behind the Attic Wall* (Avon, 1983). Twelve-year-old Maggie is sent off to creepy Uncle Morris.

Deborah and James Howe, *Bunnicula* (Avon, 1979). A vegetarian vampire bunny? Why not! The follow-up is *What Eric Knew.*

Angela Sommer-Bodenburg, *My Friend the Vampire* (Pocket Books, 1984). A nine-year-old boy makes friends with a comic vampire.

Alvin Schwartz, *Scary Stories to Tell In the Dark* (HarperCollins, 1981). Perfect for a campfire and reading aloud.

Ted Stone, *The Ghost of Peppermint Flats* (Western Producer, 1989). Fourteen scary stories by a Canadian writer.

recognized at a glance, reading speed will increase to a comfortable level for understanding the text. A reading speed of seventy words per minute (about half as fast as we normally talk) seems to be a crossover point. Children who read more slowly have to work hard at comprehension because their energy is still on decoding the words. Children who read faster find it easier to understand the meaning of the book or story.

- **Oral and silent reading** both take place at school through grade four, then the emphasis will turn to silent reading in grades five and six. Early silent reading will be no faster than reading out loud, and many children will "subvocalize" – move their lips even as they read silently. For successful readers, silent reading eventually becomes much faster than oral reading (225 to 400 words per minute silently as opposed to 125 to 175 words per minute out loud) and subvocalization is left behind. Early reading crutches like subvocalizing and using a finger pointer are not bad in themselves. There are times when we, as adults, also move our lips when reading or follow a text with our fingers. But, sooner or later, these artificial supports shouldn't be needed any more. Parents can sometimes help this along with an occasional comment during family reading time. "I bet you really don't need your finger helper for this book. The lines of print are pretty far apart." Or touch your daughter's chin when she's reading silently and the subvocalization will stop. "You'll read better if you don't move your lips" is all you need to say.

- **Reading materials**. By the end of grade three, many children will have enough confidence in their own reading ability to

Five Funny Books for Middle Schoolers

Paula Danziger, *The Cat Ate My Gymsuit* (Dell, 1974). A girl who thinks she's "a blimp" leads a student rebellion to save a popular teacher.

Martyn Godfrey, *Can You Teach Me to Pick My Nose?* (Avon, 1990). It's actually about skateboarding, but who cares?

Gordon Korman, *I Want to Go Home* (Scholastic, 1981). A hilarious story about summer camp, that will appeal to more than just the Bruno and Boots fans.

Barbara Park, *Don't Make Me Smile* (Knopf, 1981). A funny book about a boy whose parents are getting a divorce. Only Barbara Park could make it work.

Thomas Rockwell, *How to Eat Fried Worms* (Watts, 1973). The title says it all.

pass beyond favourite books and familiar material. Your grade two child wants to read about herself, even in the guise of Franklin the turtle. Your grade four child is more willing to read about astronauts, even though she isn't one, or racing cars, even though she's not old enough to drive one. Your child will begin using books not just to understand the world around her, but to extend that world. Books offer more than just stories. They are tools that your curious child can use to explore the whole universe.

By grade four, pictures will be less important than words in the books your child reads. The books themselves will be longer – "chapter books" is the school term – and reading will stretch over several sittings.

By grade five, many novels will have no illustrations at all, or perhaps only a few at the beginning of chapters. Your child will no longer need line drawings to appreciate Louise Fitzhugh's *Harriet the Spy* or the Nancy Drew mysteries.

Good Programs at School

Your child's school should still be working to turn your child into an independent reader. Though instruction in phonics and "word attack" skills is usually finished in grade three, the job of encouraging reading goes on. Good schools will use a number of techniques and approaches to consolidate basic reading skills and to promote wide, independent reading for their students.

In the classroom, the teacher should still be reading out loud, just as you are, so the kids can hear the language of more sophisticated works. Robert Munsch's books, Ted Staunton's Green Apple Street Blues books and the various Ramona novels are popular with teachers for reading with the class in grades three and four. In grades four and five, books by authors like Judy Blume, Martyn Godfrey, E.L Konigsburg, and many other writers can be read aloud.

At other times, when the kids read on their own or in groups, the works tend to be shorter and simpler. Your child can always read more difficult books when an adult is around to help. The difference in reading comes to about two grade levels. If your child has an average fourth grade reading ability, she will be more comfortable with grade three level books when reading on her own, but can probably understand a grade five level book when someone is reading with her. The ordinary fourth-grader, for instance, would have trouble reading Donald Sobol's popular *The Great Brain* books by herself because of sentence length and some difficult vocabulary. But she can easily enjoy the books when they're read to her, or when she reads along with the teacher.

Classroom teachers begin shifting their emphasis away from reading towards writing in grades four and five. This shift makes the school library and the teacher-librarian even more important in encouraging outside reading. Your child needs more than just a classroom library with its handful of books. She needs a good-sized school library with several thousand titles, from simple novels to detailed non-fiction books on insects or space flight. Your child is naturally curious. The library should have books and magazines to allow her to explore the full range of her interests.

I wrote in Chapter 3 about the importance of the whole school being involved in a reading program. This involvement is especially important to prevent grade four slump. An excellent school provides for silent reading time and for reading buddies to help kids who are falling behind. An excellent school offers chances for children to use reading in plays, or dramatizations, or the

Computer Software for Reading

Reading isn't just books — it's everything, including computer games. Some of these games are virtually skill-building lessons in themselves. All are much more sophisticated than anything available five years ago.

Mickey's ABC, for beginning readers, introduces letters and easy words, complete with Mickey's voice and music. Ages two to five.

Where in the World is Carmen Sandiego. One of a series of excellent computer games which require reading, writing, and thinking. Great graphics. Not for beginners. Ages six to twelve.

Reading and Me. Fine graphics and simulated talking with a dozen games for beginning readers. Ages four to seven.

Kid Works. A talking story-writer with a graphics program. Your child can write and illustrate her own story, then hear it read back. Ages four to eight.

Midnight Rescue. An arcade game with lots of reading and thinking. Ages seven to ten.

Children's Writing and Publishing Centre. A good, easy word-processing program to make everything from novels to newspapers.

Nancy Drew and The Hardy Boys

When these books began back in the twenties, no one could have anticipated that they would survive quite so long. The writing is uneven, the plots go *clunk* far too often, and the dialogue is from a B-movie. But still the books have some appeal.

In 1986, Simon and Schuster decided that an update was in order, so they created The Hardy Boys Files and The Nancy Drew Files. While the original book at least had some charm, these new volumes marry the worst of the Hardy boys to the worst of the Sweet Valley High genre. Best to stick to the originals.

morning announcements. An excellent school has book fairs and book exchanges and visits to the public library to encourage children to get books from a wide variety of sources. In some schools, I've seen labs with twenty computers at which kids not only read but write – and computers are great for promoting both skills. But an excellent school reading program does not require expensive electronics to be successful. It requires commitment.

In grades three and four, many schools test students for their reading and math skills. All the children in a class or a school will take two hours or more to do the Gates MacGinite or one of the dozens of other reading tests available. These tests usually have a vocabulary section and then a set of short passages with questions to measure reading comprehension. Your child will have to do the required reading, look at the choices, and mark the right answer with a pencil on a "bubble sheet" to be computer scored. A few weeks later, the results come back to the teacher or the school. In Canada, the scoring will assign a "grade level" reading ability for each student. It shows how well your child reads in comparison with a national average or norm.

The results of such tests can serve as a school report card – just how well is your child's school doing in building reading skills? In Hamilton, Ontario, for instance, weak reading scores at inner city schools resulted in extra teachers, smaller classes, and better libraries for those schools that most needed them. In addition, many boards and districts use these standardized reading tests as a first screening to determine which students need extra help. So long as the tests are followed by individualized testing and teacher consultation, they are a good way to start identifying children with reading problems.

But testing in itself is not an answer. The results can sometimes be quite inaccurate if your child doesn't know how to pace the test, or puts the pencil marks in the wrong bubbles, or maybe just feels sick or upset on the day of the test. Even when the results are accurate, few teachers can individualize their programs enough to make much use of the information that comes back. The fact that your child might be stronger in vocabulary and weaker in comprehension, or vice versa, means little for most children in terms of what happens in the classroom. The overall quality of the school reading program is what makes the difference.

Use Boredom

"Mom, I'm bored" is the common refrain of the middle school child. I remember throwing that whine at my own mother back in the 1950s. Children are wonderfully energetic and easily bored. In fact, the brighter the child, the more often she'll complain. This is natural.

So is the proper reply: "So find yourself something to do," as you continue reading or cooking or writing a report.

Don't rush out to rent a video, or buy a new computer game, or even pull out a book for your child. Boredom can be remarkably productive – when your child learns to deal with it. And your child will learn to deal with it only if given a chance to do so. If you intervene too much, you will short-circuit your child's own imagination and resources.

The media and the toy manufacturers all want your child to live a frantic life. They want her to be a consumer, a viewer, a kid constantly searching for new products to fill the void of boredom. If you allow it, these high-profit forces will raise your child for you. They will produce an adult who cannot relax, who can't find peace within herself so she seeks to buy it at the local tavern, at the drugstore or at Eaton's.

This is no legacy for your child. You must take control, ironically, by being laissez-faire. That

Want to Create A Kid's Book?

Creating a children's book isn't nearly as simple as you might think. Often it involves years of writing, rewriting, editing, creating and arranging illustrations, as well as testing it on young readers – all before the final book sees print.

If you are still interested, you might consider joining CANSCAIP, the Canadian Society of Children's Authors, Illustrators and Performers. There is one category of membership for working professionals; a "friends" category for teachers and aspiring creators. CANSCAIP offers a quarterly newsletter, a directory of members, exhibitions and performances, regular meetings in Toronto and Vancouver, and a yearly conference on writing and illustrating for children. Write: CANSCAIP, P.O. Box 280, Station L, Toronto, ON, M6E 4Z2.

Book Reviews of Kids' Books

Parents who want to get hold of the best new books for their children will have to rely on a knowledgeable bookseller, teacher, or librarian – or read reviews themselves. While some of the big daily papers have regular children's book reviewers, most newspapers tend to give kids' books a quick once-over a few weeks before Christmas. For more detailed reviews, check:

Quill and Quire: the monthly news journal of the book trade reviews almost all new Canadian books and many imports as well.

Children's Choices of Canadian Books (P.O. Box 6133, Station J, Ottawa, Ontario K2A 1T2) offers an interesting approach – kids reviewing kids' books. Often insightful and always dead-on in terms of popularity.

Canadian Children's Literature and *CM* are both primarily for teachers and librarians, but both offer reliable reviews of new books. The most readable American reviewing journal is *The Horn Book*.

Morningside on CBC radio features a regular panel on kids' books. Great suggestions, so keep a pencil in hand while listening.

wonderful French phrase literally translates as "leave to do,'" but I prefer the translation "free to be." Your child needs quiet time simply *to be,* to be herself, or engage her fantasies, to read and think, or just to be bored. To provide this freedom in our society, you must take action – turn off the TV, put away the videos, unplug the Nintendo, turn off the stereo.

Your child will amaze you. She'll read, or draw, or write her own book. She'll play fantasy games with neighbourhood kids. She'll design her own Hallowe'en costume, or turn scraps of wood into an airplane, or learn to make shadow pictures on the wall. But only if she has the freedom to be bored for a while first.

What to Read

The best phrase I've heard to describe the reading habits of children in grades three to five is "erratic independence." At this age, your child's reading will run from picture books to *Maclean's* magazine, often with no discernible pattern. And that's fine.

One new influence on your child's reading is her friends. If "all the kids'" are reading Judy Blume or Steve Jackson or Eric Wilson, your child will, too. If "all the kids" have been hooked on some series like Teenage Mutant Ninja Turtles or Encyclopedia Brown or The Babysitters' Club, then your child will want to read some, too.

Just don't spend all *your* time satisfying your child's peer group. You, too, should enjoy what you read with your child. The books she reads now are longer, so she won't be going through 300 a year any more. Try to make sure the ones you read together are worth the effort. A book like Daniel Manus Pinkwater's *The Snarkout Boys and the Avocado of Death* offers delights for you and your child both. But don't waste too much of your family reading time on the likes of the Sweet Valley High novels, unless your child is really determined to do so. There are many books that appeal to middle school children without pandering to them.

This age is often an excellent time to begin exploring more non-fiction. If your child is developing a special interest in baseball or ballet or bugs, you'll find non-fiction or 'information,' books at the library on all these topics. By zeroing in on your child's interests, you can show her that books offer far more than just stories.

How you read with your child depends really on what you choose to read together. Chances are your child will need some help starting off Louise Fitzhugh's *Harriet the Spy* to deal with some of the vocabulary and get her involved in the story. On the other hand, most nine-year-olds can sail through Beverly Cleary's *Henry Huggins* with little help at all from a parent. You should still be there – to listen to the reading and to talk about the book – but your child will likely do most of the actual reading herself. This is not the time to walk away from your child and her books; it's time to begin defining a new role that will involve you in a different way – listening more than reading aloud. As your child gets older and more independent, books will become some of the common ground you both have for conversation. Start staking out that territory now, and stay involved in your child's reading for life.

I've listed some of the best books for young readers in the sidebars to this chapter. Your local bookstore brings in new books all the time. Your public library and your child's school library will have hundreds more, new and old. Enjoy reading as many as you can. Together.

Twelve Must-have Books for Your Middle School Child's Bookshelf

Judy Blume, *Tales of a Fourth Grade Nothing* (Dell, 1972). Full of nine-year-old angst and the problems of an annoying two-year-old brother named Fudge, but warm, funny, and entertaining. A modern classic.

Roch Carrier, *The Hockey Sweater and Other Stories* (Tundra, 1984). This classic Canadian short story comes in picture book form for younger readers. A longer, mostly print book, it will appeal to grade fours and up.

Beverly Cleary. If your child has read *Ramona* (Avon, 1952), try the slightly harder *Henry Huggins* (Avon, 1950), or the harder still *Dear Mr. Henshaw* (Dell Yearling, 1983) about divorce and adjusting to a new school.

Roald Dahl, *Charlie and the Chocolate Factory* (Penguin, 1964). The bizarre story of Charlie and Willie Wonka by the British writer became a cute movie with Gene Wilder. You can use the film to spur reading of the book.

Louise Fitzhugh, *Harriet the Spy* (HarperCollins, 1964). A modern classic about a little girl who wants to be a writer.

Jean Little, *Lost and Found* (Penguin, 1985). The easiest-to-read book by Canada's most beloved children's writer. A touching story about a girl who finds a stray dog and learns about love, loneliness and responsibility.

Daniel Manus Pinkwater, *The Snarkout Boys and the Avocado of Death* (NAL, 1982). A zany mystery-adventure, amusing for both adult and child.

Mordecai Richler, *Jacob Two-Two Meets the Hooded Fang* (Bantam, 1975). Some have called this book mean-spirited, but young readers find it engaging, funny and scary. It's a winner.

Mary Rodgers, *Freaky Friday* (HarperCollins, 1972). Imagine a young girl becoming her mother. Funny, well-written and insightful.

Donald J. Sobol, *Encyclopedia Brown* (Bantam, 1963). Over a dozen books in this series of simple mysteries solved by a young detective named Leroy "Encyclopedia" Brown.

Ted Staunton, *Maggie and Me* (KidsCan, 1986). A funny, endearing story of Maggie and Cyril, who are constantly in and out of trouble.

E.B. White, *Charlotte's Web* (HarperCollins, 1952). Charlotte the Spider and Wilbur the Pig have become justly famous in this wonderful, warm story. By grade three or four, your child should be ready for the original – so long as she has your help.

CHAPTER 7

The Proficient Reader: Ages Eight to Twelve

This should be a golden age for your child as a reader – a time when he'll read widely on his own, yet still need your approval and still value what you have to say. If your child is a fluent reader by now, he will want to read everything, and likely will. He'll move from Bruce Coville's *My Teacher Is an Alien* to the Hardy Boys to comic books to Tolkien's *The Lord of the Rings* with absolutely no sense that one is much different in quality from another. He'll read at breakfast and in bed, on the bus and in the car, and sometimes for an hour or more with a flashlight after you say, "Lights out."

Of course, there is no chronological age when your child becomes a proficient reader. It's a matter of skill and attitude. When he's mastered the basics and brought his silent reading speed up to around 200 words a minute, when his recognition vocabulary is verging on adult levels and he truly enjoys reading, then your child is a proficient reader. This stage can come any time between the ages of seven and thirteen.

Unfortunately, some children never reach proficiency or are delayed trying to get there. The causes are many – from grade four slump,

The Newbery Awards

These American awards for the "best" children's books go back to 1922. Here are some selections from the winners' list:

1923: Hugh Lofting, *Voyages of Doctor Dolittle* (Dell).

1944: Esther Forbes, *Johnny Tremaine* (Dell).

1961: Scott O'Dell, *Island of the Blue Dolphins* (Dell).

1963: Madeleine L'Engle, *A Wrinkle in Time* (Dell).

1968: E.L. Konigsburg, *From the Mixed Up Files of Mrs. Basil E. Frankweiler* (Aladdin).

1970: W.H. Armstrong, *Sounder* (Harper-Collins).

1975: Virginia Hamilton, *M.C. Higgins the Great* (Macmillan).

1977: Mark Taylor, *Roll of Thunder, Hear My Cry* (Penguin).

1981: Katherine Paterson, *Jacob Have I Loved* (HarperCollins).

1986: Patricia MacLachlan, *Sarah Plain and Tall* (HarperCollins).

1990: Lois Lowry, *Number the Stars* (Dell).

1991: Jerry Spinelli, *Maniac Magee* (Little, Brown).

to boredom, to distraction, to physical problems, to emotional turmoil in the family. If your child seems to be having trouble reaching the stage of proficiency that allows easy reading for enjoyment, I suggest you skip to Chapters 10 and 11 to try to understand the problem. The remainder of this chapter talks about the parents' role for children who already read quite well.

Your New Role

When your child has become a proficient reader, he no longer needs your help to sound out the tough words or to explain those bits of history or foreign culture that were stumbling blocks in the past. He'll be reading so many books so quickly that the questions get lost in the speed of it all. Your child will likely be satisfied with a superficial sense of the plot or the ideas in a book. He'll figure out difficult vocabulary from context and probably not care much how the word might be pronounced. When your child stops long enough to ask you what a word means, you may both have to look it up.

But you still have a vital role in his reading. Your child still needs to talk about books he's read. You can still use his reading to begin more general talks about life, the universe, and the one or two other things in between. And you are still important in shaping and expanding your child's reading experience.

The three Rs remain vital, even if your child seems to be a very accomplished reader. The best way to avoid the boredom and disinterest that afflicts so many teenagers in grade nine is to keep on with the basics right through elementary school: read with your child every day; reach into your wallet to buy a wide selection of books and magazines for your child; rule the television so there's time for reading to happen.

Your family reading will have changed by now. Your child will be reading for up to an hour after you leave the bedroom, and maybe another hour during the day. By grade nine, the real readers will read well over ten hours a week. So when you drop into the bedroom, the page or two you read together won't have much connection to the page or two you read the night before.

Read the page anyway. Reading the page aloud slows down the pace of your child's reading so he can ask questions, or get the meaning of that word he skipped over, or enjoy the flavour of the prose. Reading the page aloud gives you the chance to ask an important question before you begin: "What happened in the story since the last time we read?" This gives your child a chance to explain what's going on (an important skill in itself), or to say why he changed books ("Aw, Mom, it got so boring"), or to draw you into the reading ("Let me read you this funny part back on page, uh, I'll find it.")

Some children at this age will begin to protest: "Dad, I can read better than you now." Or they'll pretend independence: "I don't need to be read to any more. That's for kids." Or they'll find the idea of sitting down with you to read for half an hour just "gross." I suggest that you not give in too easily to these protests. Try to make a deal that keeps family reading time going. Here are some answers you might try:

- "Right, you are an excellent reader. So why don't you read to me for fifteen minutes?"

- "Let me read just a couple of pages so I can see what the book's about."

- "Okay, why don't I just look through the book for a minute and then we can talk about it?"

- "How about I read the narration and you read the dialogue. It'll be fun."

- "Okay, so let me read you just a page from this novel your Mom and I are reading."

As your child approaches the teenage years, his reading will necessarily become more private. When my kids started reading Ruth Bell's *Changing Bodies, Changing Lives*, they didn't want me reading aloud the descriptive sections on sex or making out. But we could continue our reading together by opening a novel or a comic book that was a bit less emotionally charged.

The fallback position, of course, is to stop the reading and simply talk about a book. Talking is not as good as reading out loud together, but it is better than making reading entirely a private and lonely experience. Statisticians tell us that the average parent engages in real conversation with a teenage child for less than four minutes a week. By sitting down with your son or daughter to talk about what they're reading, you'll triple that time with hardly any work at all. If your daughter is reading Judy Blume's *Forever*, you have a wonderful chance to talk about dating – both hers and yours. If your son is reading Brian Doyle's *Up to Low*, you have a chance to talk about anger and violence in the book and in your son's life. In fact, almost any book gives you a chance to talk about something and that talking will help carry your child through the danger time still to come.

What's Happening at School

In the senior elementary grades, "reading" turns into "English" or "language arts." This doesn't mean that reading has stopped, only that the emphasis has changed to writing and responding. Your child's class might all be reading *The Diary of Anne Frank*, or *Jacob Have I Loved*, or *Mama's Going to Buy You a Mocking Bird*, but the reading will mostly be silent and often will occur at home. Time in school will be spent discussing the characters, or the turns of plot, or trying to understand concepts like theme and irony.

Five Heartbreakers

For senior elementary kids who don't mind a good cry:

Betsy Byars, *The Summer of the Swans* (Penguin, 1970). An earnest fourteen-year-old on the day her retarded brother gets lost.

Sylvia McNicoll, *Blueberries and Whipped Cream* (Gage, 1987). A dying mother and a sensitive girl. Won't leave a dry eye.

Katherine Paterson, *Bridge to Terabithia* (HarperCollins, 1977) offers a tale of friendship, courage, and long suffering. Her *Jacob Have I Loved* (HarperCollins, 1980) is fast becoming a classic.

Cynthia Voigt, *Homecoming* (Atheneum, 1981). An independent thirteen-year-old saves her family after their mother deserts them.

Assuming your child is a reader, he'll have to put his energy into the writing part of language arts. Senior elementary students move quickly from single paragraphs to longer reports and presentations. The books they read are really material for a writing program that can range from reader-response journals (a diary for recording your child's ideas after each chapter) to book reports.

A good senior elementary English program will also offer any number of other means of responding to books – making videos, doing dramatizations, recording radio plays, interviewing the characters, perhaps even interviewing you. The only limit is the imagination of your child's teacher (if your child is still in a single classroom) or teachers (if the school is on a rotary system where kids move to different rooms for different subjects). An excellent school will offer all sorts of outreach programs – from trips to the local theatre, to public library visits, to school musicals, to being a reading buddy for a younger student.

Your child's school should expect and support a certain amount of reading at home – at least a book a month. How your child reports back on that reading is up to the teacher, but you should check up on those expectations on parents' night. Your child will also be getting nightly homework, which should amount to at least an hour a night by grade eight. Some of this will be in geography, history, math, and health, but much will be writing for language arts.

The key for supporting student work through the senior elementary and early high school grades is simple: the kitchen table.

I imagine you're looking strangely at the page now, wondering if there's been some strange typographical error. Let me repeat: the key to helping your child through school from age ten to age sixteen is the kitchen table (or its equivalent). Homework – reports, math problems,

Five Page-Turners

For senior elementary kids who want a gripping story:

John Bellairs, *The House with a Clock in Its Walls* (Dell, 1973) and many other titles. Spooky and ghoulish but always fun.

Bruce Coville, *My Teacher is an Alien* (Minstrel, 1989). Just what we always suspected. Funny and ironic, but exciting.

John Christopher, *The White Mountains* (Macmillan, 1967). Really junior sci-fi adventure, but it works.

Claire Mackay, *Mini Bike Hero* (Scholastic, 1974) is a classic sports story, while her *Minerva Program* (Lorimer, 1984) makes computers exciting.

For the Kid Who Reads Too Much

Some kids can spend too much time reading, just as they can spend too much time watching TV or playing sports. To keep a balance, try these:

• Turn books into activities. Sci-fi can spark an interest in astronomy if you're there to give a push.

• Turn reading into writing. Don't just read another Sweet Valley High, write one.

• Sports. Maybe you've been through soccer and Little League with dismal results, but what about less obvious sports that your child might enjoy — archery, croquet, badminton? These can provide other avenues of success for the bookish child.

• Games. Good readers frequently excel at Scrabble or Trivial Pursuit or computer games that are language-based.

French verbs, essay questions – should be done at the kitchen table or some other central location in the house. Homework should be worked on someplace where you or another adult will be near by.

Teachers stumbled across the "kitchen table" phenomenon when they went looking for explanations of student achievement. In recent years, immigrant children have been outperforming Canadian-born children in virtually every subject area, even in English at senior grades. Teachers wondered why. Obviously, parents couldn't be doing the work for their kids; the parents themselves often had a hard time with our language. Social and family attitudes account for some of the difference, but hardly all of it. What observation showed was this: the immigrant children were doing their homework with their family physically in the room. They weren't told, "Go to the bedroom and do your homework." They were expected to sit at the kitchen table, or dining room table, or counter in the store, and get on with their work. This accomplished two things: it provided an adult to show interest, supervise work, and help if help was needed; and it said that school work was important to the whole family.

I am not suggesting that parents should stick their noses into homework, any more than they should stick their noses into their children's reading at this stage. But I would suggest that you try to create an environment that supports and gives importance to schoolwork. And that you find a way to make homework a social experience, just like reading.

In my house, when I was growing up in the 1950s, homework was done in the dining room with a vigour that left permanent scratches in my mother's cherry wood dining room table. To this day, I prefer to work close to other people. My office is located on the second floor, just over the kitchen, where I can hear everyone else even as I type this page. My step-daughter, Emma, still prefers to do her university work at our dining room table, even though she has her own room and her own computer. For both of us, there is something comforting about taking on a big project with other, supportive people around. I suggest that every family give it a try.

Guiding Your Child's Reading

A portion of your child's reading in the senior elementary grades will be for school, and will be serious literature, books that require reasonable thought and a carefully written-out responses. But your child should also be reading much more, both in school and at home. He should be going through books, magazines, short stories, poetry, essays, the great classics – and junk.

Yes, I'm in favour of junk reading. Every reader I know reads junk: cheap mysteries, *Cosmopolitan*, Harlequin romances, true-crime stories, *The National Enquirer*. Once we've become proficient readers, we'll read everything. I can't stand in line at the supermarket without picking up those newspapers with headlines like "My child had two heads – but I loved them anyway."

Your children should be allowed their fair share of junk reading, too. No child was ever helped to become a reader for life by being force-fed the Bible, or New Age pamphlets, or Immanuel Kant. No child was ever hurt by reading a half-dozen Sweet Valley High romances.

But I have seen children hurt – intellectually and emotionally – by a steady diet of junk which stretched over a number of years. In my creative writing class, I can tell the girls who have read too many Harlequins by their breathless prose and impossible characters. Even worse, I can see them dreaming about the young doctor with whom they'll fall in love on their vacation in Fiji. The real world, I'm afraid, rarely works like that.

Your job, as the parent of a proficient reader,

Junior Sci-Fi and Fantasy

In grades seven and eight some kids get hooked on this genre. Try these titles for starters:

Monica Hughes, *Ring-Rise Ring-Set* (Heinemann, 1982). A fifteen-year-old girl runs from her domed city to be rescued by "Ekoes," whose Native Indian ways may save the planet.

C.S. Lewis, Chronicles of Narnia, including *The Lion, the Witch and the Wardrobe* (HarperCollins, 1950). Your kids don't have to know that this seven-volume series is a Christian allegory in fantasy form.

John Wyndham, *Day of the Triffids* (Penguin, 1951) with walking vegetables or *The Chrysalids* (Penguin, 1955) which is a more sophisticated story of human mutants.

T.H. White, *The Sword in the Stone* (HarperCollins, 1975). A King Arthur fantasy with an orphan boy and Merlin the Magician. It became a Disney animated film that many kids love.

is to encourage variety. For a boy who's reading his seventh Steve Jackson and Ian Livingstone fantasy novel, it's quite fair to say, "I don't want to hear any more of that tonight. Let's start this book by Martyn Godfrey." Sure, there may be complaints, but you've made your point. Reading time is shared time; it's disposition is up to you, too.

A wonderful aspect of the senior elementary school reader is suggestibility. At this age, unlike the teen reader, children still respond to our likes and dislikes. As parents, using our judgement and the ideas from this book, we can promote the reading of good books and discourage a steady diet of junk.

Try these techniques:

- "Okay, you can take out only three books on your library card. How about one Choose Your Own Adventure and this Gordon Korman book that I think you'll like. Then you pick one more."

- "I'll pay for any reasonable book, but if you want another Babysitter's Little Sister book, you buy it yourself."

- "I don't care if the kid next door has read twenty Sweet Valley High books, it's time for you to read something with a little more challenge in it. Your cousin Kate recommended . . ."

- "I was at the library today, and Mrs. Frost said that somebody who reads Bruce Coville all the time, as you do, might also like this book . . ."

Most kids will get out of a particular reading rut after a few months all by themselves. With a little encouragement and nudging from you, the move to other, more varied books will come sooner.

Four top Canadian Authors for Middle School Kids

- Martyn Godfrey is an Alberta writer with a long list of sci-fi, adventure and humorous novels to his credit. Weaker readers will enjoy *More Than Weird*; stronger readers will like the excitement in *The Vandarian Incident* or the humour in *Baseball Crazy*.

- Jean Little is one of Canada's most honoured writers for children. Her novel *Mamma's Going to Buy You a Mockingbird* has become a Canadian classic; her autobiography, *Little by Little*, and its sequel, *Stars Come Out Within*, are honest, inspiring books.

- Gordon Korman began writing novels when he was still a grade seven student in Thornhill, Ontario. His funny novels about Bruno and Boots made his reputation with kids. Newer works like *Radio Fifth Grade* and *The Zucchini Warriors* are also funny but more sophisticated.

- Brian Doyle of Ottawa has captured historical moments, racial conflict, and the real life of young people in a number of award-winning novels. *Up to Low, Angel Square*, and *Easy Street* are often studied in grades seven and eight. His recent novel, *Covered Bridge*, has been well received.

What makes a good book for the proficient reader? Pretty much the same qualities as those that make a good book for an adult – respect for the reader and the subject of the book, the artistry or clarity of the writing, the capacity to entertain and inform, the honesty of the author's vision. Not all good books get the sophisticated covers and packaging that make them look appealing on the library shelf.

Here, teachers, librarians, and bookstore proprietors can be a big help to you. They can suggest books that have been reviewed favourably, but which your child might not choose himself. Jean Little's *Mama's Going To Buy You a Mockingbird* will not jump off the shelf with a snazzy cover, and, like many good books, it's more expensive than an American pulp novel. But it's a fine book and deserves reading.

Your child has no easy way of knowing this. He's more likely to judge a book by its cover, which was done by an artist who may have only skimmed through the book. Or he'll read the back-cover blurb, written by an editor at the publishing house. Or he'll listen to the recommendations of Johnny from down the street. None of these will say much about the actual quality of a book.

Part of your job, as a parent, is to encourage your child to read more than that which is immediately appealing. If you can get advice from teachers or librarians or bookstore owners, that's wonderful. If you come across recommendations in the newspaper or the other media, those will also be helpful. But often you won't have much to go on when you're at the library or bookstore. Let me suggest the "Page 40 Test" for those times.

Expand Their Universe

When young children begin to read, they start with picture books and then move on to longer stories. In both cases, the genre is fiction.

The Page 40 Test

This quick test works for both adult and children's fiction – and can be done by you and your child together.

- Open the book to page 40. By page 40, the author has got the story going, the editor has relaxed his blue pencil, and you'll get a real sense of the bottom-line quality of the book.

- Read the page carefully. Listen to it. Is the prose lively and interesting? Is the dialogue realistic? Are you inclined to read on?

- Or is the prose leaden and dull? Is the dialogue the kind you'd expect on a soap opera but would never hear in real life? Is the book obviously moralizing or patronizing? Do you really want to read on?

Two minutes spent on page 40 could save you and your child many hours reading a lousy book.

A Little History . . .

Pierre Berton, *Adventures in Canadian History* (McClelland & Stewart, 1991, etc.) A series of short books, well told and well researched by Canada's famous adult historian.

Barbara Greenwood, *A Question of Loyalty* (Scholastic, 1984). A young girl has to decide whether to give refuge to a British Loyalist soldier.

John Ibbitson, *1812* (Maxwell Macmillan, 1991). A young man caught in the War of 1812. Gripping adventure and good history.

Janet Lunn, *The Root Cellar* (Penguin, 1985). A little mystery, a ghost or two, and a bit of history set near Kingston, Ontario.

Anne Frank, *Anne Frank: The Diary of a Young Girl* (Pocket, 1947). A classic, Anne Frank's account of her experience during the Holocaust is both gripping and touching.

Barbara Smucker, *Underground to Canada* (Penguin, 1977). A serious story that follows the slave Julilly from when she is sold in Virginia to her reunion with her mother in Canada.

Teachers and librarians estimate that only four percent of what young children read comes from the "information books" or non-fiction section. Yet adult readers buy more non-fiction than they do novels.

These last elementary school years are when the crossover begins. They are a great time to show your child that there's much more to books than stories. There are wonderful books on every subject from astronomy to zoology, from David Suzuki's books on science to Camilla Gryski's books on string figures. These books are fun, activity-based, and beautifully illustrated.

Instead of reading a chapter from a novel, why not cut two pieces of string and try one of the native string figures explained in Gryski's *Cat's Cradle, Owl's Eyes*? Instead of reading two pages of a story, why not set up a terrarium as outlined in *Scienceworks* from the Ontario Science Centre? Kids who turn away from fiction at this age can still get excited about many other kinds of books and reading.

The key, of course, is to tie your suggestions to your child's interests. There is no sense pushing a book on bicycles to a girl who's wild about horses. But it makes very good sense to take a son in Little League to the bookstore for a book on the history of the game; or the girl who makes model airplanes out to buy the Scientific American's *Great Model Airplane Book*. Libraries are especially useful for non-fiction books. Bookstores rarely have enough children's non-fiction to zero in on your child's interests (save perhaps baseball and horses), but they can order any book you discover elsewhere – from something on scuba diving to any number of books on stamp collecting.

Magazines and newspapers should also be part of your child's expanded universe. Many newspapers have a children's page on Saturday, like the Toronto *Star*'s "Starship", which tries to promote children's reading and knowledge of current issues. And the range of children's magazines is enormous – from the still-funny *Mad Magazine* to *Teen Generation* and *Nintendo Power*. If some of them grab your child's interest, subscribe to keep the magazine coming.

Let Them Explore

The proficient reader will read everything, including books that might make you uncomfortable. Eleven- and twelve-year olds, especially, look for gritty titles that measure up to what they see on television and in movies.

Trust your child. It's unlikely that he will ever bring home one of those steamy pseudo-Victorian porn novels you find at the corner store. But your ten-year-old son might want to read a title like M.E. Kerr's *Dinky Hocker Shoots Smack!* or your eleven-year-old daughter might bring home Judy Blume's *Forever*. Don't panic. Children are naturally curious about everything from sex to volcanoes to street gangs. If you make a big deal about the sex in *Forever*, you'll not only distort what the book is really about but you'll give undue attention to material that probably isn't that interesting to an elementary school reader. I'd worry far more about what's available on your television, or via your neighbour's satellite dish. One survey in New York suggested that a quarter of the children in grade eight had already seen an X-rated movie. Far better that they should read about sex presented with some honesty in a young adult novel.

Reading and Writing

Especially in senior elementary school, reading and writing should be interconnected. If you've done your job, your child is already on his way to being a lifelong reader. But our society demands that successful individuals also be skilled writers.

Evaluating Non-Fiction

How good are the non-fiction books your child might want to buy or borrow? Evaluating them isn't as simple as the "page 40 test." You have to look through the whole book and try to answer some questions.

- Who's it for? Is the book really written for kids? How hard is it to read? How complicated are the sentences? How difficult is the vocabulary?

- Is it for reading or reference? Don't buy a reference book like *Mammals of America* and expect it to be read. But no kid could resist a grabber like *Strange But True Sports Stories*.

- Are the illustrations appropriate? Older kids frequently prefer line drawings to beautiful colour prints. For some books, say, one on bike repair, good illustrations are vital.

- Is the writing clear and interesting? Try reading a paragraph to get a feel for the author's style.

Five Best Magazines for Middle School Kids

Boy's Life and *The Guider*. The Boy Scout magazine and its Girl Guide equivalent. Both well done.

Cricket. The Literary Magazine for Children. Sort of *Harper's* for the young set, but it also publishes stories by young writers.

Mad. It's funny, irreverent, and obnoxious — just as it was when you read it.

National Geographic World. Photography as slick as its adult counterpart. A little more difficult than *Owl*.

Sports Illustrated for Kids. So well done that its adult counterpart could learn a few things. Kid focused. Great photography.

Without pushing too hard, you can tie reading and writing together at home for your child.

- Write letters. To Grandma, to the author of a book your child enjoyed (send it to the publisher), to the newspaper, to the prime minister (no postage required). If that expensive squirt gun stopped working, send a letter of complaint to the manufacturer. Writing, like reading, will empower your child.

- Write stories. Your child is probably writing stories at school. Why not do one at home, together? Naturally your child will end up as the central character. Just add the real-life settings around you and let your imagination go.

- Write scripts. If your family has a video camera, try a family-written, family-acted drama. Write and polish the script before you start.

- Write feelings. As your child becomes more of his own private person, he might want to keep a journal or diary. Why not encourage it? But remember that you're not allowed to read it unless you're invited.

Don't spend a great deal of time worrying about spelling, grammar, and punctuation. First we write, then we go back and fix. If you have a home computer, a spell checker will correct many mistakes with hardly any effort. But no computer will ever get your child to write if every word has to be spelled perfectly and every comma put in just the right place. Research has shown that the average student makes three to four errors per hundred words from grade six to grade twelve. The rate stays the same but the errors become more sophisticated. For that progress to happen, your child should feel secure and confident about writing, and have an audience to admire the work.

That audience is you. Be full of praise. Don't push too hard for corrections. Not every letter should be sent; not every story deserves to be printed up. So always start with a few responses like "That's wonderful, James. I never knew you had such an imagination." Then you might suggest: "Do you want to fix the spelling and print the story as a book?" Or, "Maybe before we mail this to the mayor we should look up a couple of the words and print it again."

Enjoy These Years

Soon your child will become a teenager and enter a world that our society has cut off both from childhood and adult life. Your daughter will be full of secrets; your son full of swaggering intensity. For now, your child is in a golden age. Enjoy it while it lasts.

Twelve Must-have Books for Your Proficient Reader's Bookshelf

Judy Blume, *Are You There, God? It's Me, Margaret* (Dell, 1970). If your child liked *Tales of a Fourth Grade Nothing*, this is the natural extension of young, middle-class angst.

Eleanor Coerr, *Sadako and the Thousand Paper Cranes* (Putnam, 1977). A beautiful, sensitive book about a twelve-year-old girl who dies of leukaemia as a result of the bombing of Hiroshima.

Brian Doyle, *Up to Low* (Douglas & McIntyre, 1982) and *Easy Avenue* (Douglas & McIntyre, 1988). Two award-winning novels by an Ottawa writer. Both deal with the problems of identity played out against difficult times.

Martyn Godfrey, *Here She Comes, Ms. Teeny-Wonderful* (Scholastic, 1984). This book and the other "Teeny Wonderful" books are much better than their titles – funny, meaningful, and always popular, especially with girls.

Monica Hughes, The Isis Trilogy. Every child should get a taste of sci-fi. These three books – *Guardian of Isis*, *The Isis Peddler*, and *Keeper of the Isis Light* (Hamish Hamilton, 1981, etc.) – feature a sixteen-year-old girl as their central character.

Jean Little, *Mama's Going to Buy You a Mockingbird.* (Penguin, 1984). This now-classic book by Canada's most beloved children's writer deals sensitively with how a child heals emotionally after the death of a parent.

Gordon Korman, *This Can't be Happening at Macdonald Hall* (Scholastic, 1983). This is the novel that Korman wrote when still a private school student. Its funny hijinks and lively characters, Bruno and Boots, have wide appeal.

The Canadian Junior Encyclopedia (Hurtig, 1990). Parents are frequently browbeaten into buying expensive encyclopaedias that are nothing but a waste of good money. Here's one for less than $100 that is worth every penny. Three volumes.

L.M. Montgomery, *Anne of Green Gables* (Seal, 1900). The story of spunky Anne and her family is much loved by many middle school girls, even more so since the release of the movie and TV spin-offs.

Jerry Spinelli, *Maniac Magee* (Little Brown, 1990). This novel took all the awards in 1991: a funny, exciting and moving modern legend.

David Suzuki with Barbara Hehner, *Looking at the Environment* (Stoddart, 1989). An accessible book on an important issue for the next generation by Canada's top scientist-writer. Try also his daughter Laura's series, David Suzuki Asks, Did You Know . . . (General, 1990, etc.).

J.R.R. Tolkien, *The Hobbit* (Ballantine, 1937). This fantasy classic abounds with wonderful, archetypal characters. Bilbo Baggins sets out to help dwarves recover their treasure from a dragon. A popular read among good readers in grades 7 and 8.

CHAPTER 8

The Teenage Reader

The teenage years are tough on parents. Suddenly we're cut off from our children's lives. We no longer really know their friends. We wonder what they're doing on Friday night at 2:00 AM, and we worry without the power or information to act on our worries.

But these years are also tough on the teenagers themselves. Suddenly your child discovers the opposite sex, shaving cream or lipstick, alcohol and/or drugs, Metallica or U2, pimples and the power of a driver's licence. Your child can now form her own opinions and argue hotly with yours. She is so desperately trying to define her own identity that she expends a massive amount of effort rejecting yours.

All of this begins to explain why the early teenage years are the second most dangerous time for readers. If your child has successfully weathered the grade four slump, then grades eight, nine, and ten become the years that determine whether reading will remain a big part of her life. It would be safe to say that almost two-thirds of Canadian children in middle school read widely for pleasure. After the grade nine slump, that figure has dropped to about

20 percent of the student population. In this chapter, I want to look at the reasons we're losing so many readers in high school and what you, as a parent, can do to make sure your child isn't one of the casualties.

Illiteracy and Aliteracy

The danger in adolescence is not that our children will lose their reading skills, but that they will stop using them. A fair portion of our young people – competent readers through middle school – suddenly declare that they have no time to read, or that they are too busy working, or that they read enough at school and no longer want to on their own. Their attitude towards reading goes from enthusiasm to indifference. This is what sociologist Daniel Boorstein calls "aliteracy." The term describes situations in which a child can read well enough, but can't be bothered to actually do so.

I'll use one of my grade eleven English students as an example.

"So what was the last book you read outside school, Richard?"

"Can't remember. We read something last year . . ." He searches his memory for *To Kill a Mockingbird* but can't come up with the title.

"I meant outside school."

"Not much," he says, embarrassed. "I saw a couple of videos this week and went to the movies?" Richard looks up for approval.

"Open any books?"

"School books?"

"Real books," I say.

Richard looks down at his hands.

"Read a newspaper?"

He shakes his head.

"Any magazines?"

"Well, yeah." Richard smiles, relieved. "Tom had this magazine on Guns 'N' Roses, like, so I read this thing about Slash. It was awesome."

Is Richard illiterate? Definitely not. He has no

problem with phonics, word attack skills, definitions by context, vocabulary to a grade nine level, oral fluency, or reading rate. He just doesn't read.

Richard's problem, that of aliteracy, has everyone stumped. The Southam Press management, eyeballing the graphs of falling daily newspaper readership among young people, have tried everything from pumping up the jolts in the writing of daily columnists to bringing in a new tabloid "news" paper that focuses primarily on rock stars and nightclubs. Book publishers have tried to hold onto teenage readers by offering junior versions of adult fare such as Harlequin Romances or by promoting writers such as Stephen King whose strongest appeal is to adolescents. For some teenagers, these efforts are working, but for Richard and many others, books and reading are being discarded as childhood ends.

Our teenagers didn't create this situation themselves. Many of them are victims of a campaign to commercialize all of childhood. Sometime in the 1950s, teenagers in North America became a target market – a consumer group with both money to spend and specific product demands. No other demographic group, save the truly wealthy, has as much disposable cash. Ten percent of all the young people in North America will work during adolescence for one company – McDonald's. Two-thirds of all teenagers in grades eleven and twelve will work, and 20 percent of them will work more than fifteen hours a week.

Many teenagers have been told that they don't have to worry about mortgages, health care, food on the table, family vacations, hard times, or even the cost of their own educations. Only a small portion of them will contribute earnings to their households. The rest will spend their money on specially marketed, high-profit items ranging from designer running shoes to cosmetics. No wonder our suggestible adolescents, who are pummelled by messages for Nikes, Paco Rabane and Chevrolet Berettas, spend their

Six Top Young Adult Books

Realistic, serious fiction for younger teens.

William Bell, *Absolutely Invincible* (Stoddart, 1988). A serious portrait of half a dozen sad young people fighting to be themselves.

Judy Blume, *Tiger Eyes* (Dell, 1981). More mature than her fiction for the grade five set, but very American.

Robert Cormier, *I Am the Cheese* (Dell, 1977). A gripping adventure story by the author of *The Chocolate War* (Dell, 1974). Nobody handles social terror better than Cormier.

Scott O'Dell, *Island of the Blue Dolphins* (Dell, 1960). Strong appeal for some teens. A twelve-year-old, abandoned on a Pacific island, survives and grows to womanhood.

Richard Peck, *Are You in the House Alone?* (Dell, 1976). The terror of rape, well-handled.

Sue Townsend, *The Secret Diary of Adrian Mole, Aged 13 3/4.* (Methuen, 1982). A sensation in England, both for teens and adults, with its amusing account of a gifted and ambitious young man.

money on what they're made to want instead of what they really need.

Adolescents may not see how much they need to read. Cut off from the responsibilities of adult society, they tend to ignore newspapers, many magazines, and serious literature about adult life. Told they are no longer children, they often begin to feel that their earlier reading was just childish.

To make the situation worse, there is no body of literature that appeals specifically to older teens. Every young person wants to read about kids who are somewhat older. Your grade three daughter wants to read *Tales of a Fourth Grade Nothing*, but your grade six daughter wouldn't bother. Your thirteen-year-old son will read Marilyn Halvorson's *Cowboys Don't Cry* to see what it's like to be sixteen, but your eighteen-year-old son wouldn't dream of it. Significantly, there is no body of literature about university students for high school students to read. No one has bothered to assemble such a genre, so our high school students must turn to adult books when they aren't yet adults.

Or they turn away from reading altogether.

Don't Give Up

Reading remains vital, both to our society as a whole and to our children as individuals. The twenty percent of our teenagers who survive the grade nine slump are the ones who will develop the sophisticated reading skills they need for work, community college and university. The others are losing ground in the highly competitive world our young people must enter. As parents, we want to provide the encouragement that will keep our teens reading for their own pleasure – and their own futures.

The key is the three R's, somewhat modified for your child at this age.

- Keep reading with your teenager on some kind of regular basis. You might feel awkward reading out loud to a hulking teenage boy, but there's no reason you can't pick up your son's grade eleven novel, read the backcover blurb or a page of the text, and talk about it. I know a single parent who shares every book she reads with her daughter – and asks for the same in return. The mother has read more young adult novels than I have, and enjoyed most of them. I know a family who keep their teenage son reading by making a point of talking about books at dinner – not movies or TV or school work – but books. Jewish families have long made oral reading a part of their cultural and family tradition at holidays. You can create your own reading traditions – a special reading of Dickens at Christmas, or a family gathering at which everyone writes or reads a poem about a special event. At our house, we take time to read out loud from the newspaper – everything from Ann Landers to horoscopes to outrageous editorials. Many families enjoy reading aloud a magazine quiz, or questions from a trivia book as evening entertainment. Reading will stay important to your teenager so long as it stays important to everyone.

- Keep buying books for your teenager. I've said it before: books are too special to be rolled into the weekly allowance or their purchase left to chance. Why not provide a special book allowance – and then read a portion of the purchased book yourself so you can talk with your son? Why not use the reading lists in this book to provide reading material for your teenage daughter? Tell your child she can have two books for free from the lists. Kids love the idea of getting something for nothing, and she'll probably have

Ten Worthwhile Fantasy Novels

Many of these books are part of a series, so look for authors more than titles.

Piers Anthony, *On A Pale Horse* (Ballantine, 1983).

Robert Aspirin, *Another Fine Myth* (Berkeley, 1978).

Orson Scott Card, *Seventh Son* (Tor, 1987).

Raymond E. Feist, *Magician: Apprentice* (Bantam, 1982).

Welwyn Wilton Katz, *The Third Magic* (Groundwood, 1988).

Ursula K. Le Guin, *The Wizard of Earthsea* (Puffin, 1968).

Anne McCaffrey, *Dragonflight* (Ballantine, 1968).

Terry Pratchett, *The Colour of Magic* (Penguin/ROC, 1983).

Robert Silverberg, *Lord Valentine's Castle* (HarperCollins, 1980).

J.R.R. Tolkien, *The Lord of the Rings* (Unwin, 1954).

Ten Top Sci-Fi Books

I've listed each writer's most famous title, but all these authors have a long list of good books.

Isaac Asimov, *Foundation* (Ballantine, 1951).

Ray Bradbury, *Fahrenheit 451* (Pocket Books, 1967).

David Brin, *Startide Rising* (Bantam, 1983).

Philip Jose Farmer, *Dayworld* (Ace, 1985).

William Gibson, *Neuromancer* (Ace, 1984).

Robert A. Heinlein, *Stranger in a Strange Land* (Ace, 1961).

Frank Herbert, *Dune* (Ace, 1961).

Judith Merrill, *Daughters of Earth* (Gollancz, 1968).

Spider Robinson, *Stardance* (Dial, 1979).

Fred Saberhagen, *Berserker* series (TOR, 1984).

Robert A. Wilson, *Schrodinger's Cat* (Dell, 1984).

her interest piqued enough to give the books a try. Our family always takes a trip to the bookstore and library for a book-binge before we leave for the cottage. And then we trade the best "reads" when we're on vacation, sharing the good books with each other. Our neighbours know that if they borrow a video at the library, there's a good chance their teenage daughter will also take out a book. The teenager down the street won't read her father's *Globe and Mail,* but he'll read her copy of *Now,* Toronto's entertainment paper, so they have something to talk about. The way in which you share reading with teenagers in your family's life depends on how you live. Just be sure that books aren't left out.

• Rule the TV so reading can happen. Statistically, teenagers watch less television than anyone else, but that's only because so many of their waking hours are taken up with school, jobs and friends. However the remaining hours can still be spent simply plopped in front of the tube: MuchMusic after school, *Gilligan's Island* through dinner, *Wheel of Fortune* at seven, the nightly video until news time, *Saturday Night Live,* or *Late Night with David Letterman,* or Benny Hill reruns until exhaustion . . . with the screen still going for cartoons in the morning – unless you maintain rules that shut the machine down.

Your teenage child, of course, will tell you she can read, do homework, and think about existential philosophy – all with headphones on, a Gameboy on the desk, and the TV screen five feet from her face. She's wrong. While today's children really can shut out the TV better than we could, very few can combine a passive attitude like viewing with active attitudes for reading or writing. The research is conclusive: any teenager who watches more than three hours of television a day is more likely to have problems in school, problems at home and problems as a reader. Do your teenager a favour: turn the TV off after two or three hours.

What's Happening in High School

Reading itself is not specifically taught in high school; it's simply expected. Every subject from English to calculus depends on reading – often with textbooks written at university levels of difficulty. If your child isn't reading well enough to cope, the first report card will show it. Turn to Chapters 10 and 11 for some solutions.

Most teenagers do read adequately to handle high school work. They just don't read enough. I've seen very few students who can't do the assigned reading in novels or textbooks. What the students don't do is outside reading: novels for themselves, newspapers and magazines on current events, non-fiction on anything more substantial than rock music.

Younger teens will tell you that they're too busy to read, or that they have more important things to do. Older teens will tell you they don't have time to read after juggling school, part-time jobs, homework, and a social life. Recreational reading, when it happens, is pieced into a busy schedule – a few pages on the bus, reading in the hall on a spare, a few minutes before sleep. Interestingly, some readers – the twenty percent – still manage to find more than ten hours a week to read because reading has become a habit. The aliterate teen will tell you she has no time at all.

High schools try to keep some outside reading alive through book reports or research projects, but their success is spotty. Even in English courses, the move to semestered (half-year) courses has made it more difficult to teach longer works. The

Governor General's Award Winners

These Canadian books for older readers have won the GG or its predecessor, the Canada Council Literary Award.

1991: Sarah Ellis, *Pick-Up Sticks* (Douglas & McIntyre, 1991). A bookish girl and her family in Vancouver.

1990: Michael Bedard, *Redwork* (Lester, 1990). From cockroaches to William Blake, this teen novel combines realism and magic.

1989: Diana Wieler, *Bad Boy* (Stoddart, 1989). A teenage athlete reveals his homosexuality – for more mature readers.

1988: Welwyn Katz, *The Third Magic* (Groundwood, 1988). A complex but beautifully written fantasy for bright readers.

1987: Morgan Nyerg, *Galahad Schwartz and the Cockroach Army*. (Groundwood, 1987).

1986: Janet Lunn, *Shadow in Hawthorn Bay* (Lester & Orpen Dennys, 1986).

1985: Cora Taylor, *Julie* (Western Producer, 1985).

1984: Jan Hudson, *Sweetgrass* (Tree Frog, 1984).

1983: sean o'huigin, *The Ghost Horse of the Mounties* (Black Moss, 1983).

1982: Monica Hughes, *Hunter in the Dark* (Stoddart, 1982).

1981: Monica Hughes, *The Guardian of Isis* (Hamish Hamilton, 1981).

Tools for Good Students

Dictionary. It's still the only way to really check spelling and whether you want "weather" or "whether."

Calculator. Essential for high school math courses and many science and technical courses as well.

Pocket planner. Teens don't need a leather daytimer, but they do need a handy calendar to record assignments and due-dates. Some schools have taken to issuing one free to each student.

Pencil. Don't just underline; respond to your books in the margins. Also helpful for (a) note taking, (b) multiple-choice tests, (c) rough drafts of assignments and (d) providing your phone number to certain select individuals.

Computer. I know we're talking over a thousand dollars here, but a computer really is worth the money if you can afford it. These days, spelling and grammar checkers can turn even bumbling writers into competent wordmeisters — a real plus for every subject from English to history to kinesiology. Then there are programs in math, business, science, engineering . . . the list is lengthy. Sometimes working but out-of-date computers can be bought for less than the cost of high-tech running shoes. Shop around.

typical high school English course still has an assortment of short stories, poetry, a bit of Shakespeare, perhaps one other play, an essay or two, and a novel – but rarely more than one novel. There just isn't time to cover any more in a twenty-week course. As a result, your child may come home bent over with required work for presentations or reports, but she's unlikely to appear with piles of books to read.

For high school students to survive the demands of the senior grades – and to keep some time for their own reading – they have to learn to read efficiently for school. Good schools take time to discuss reading and study skills in grade nine English, history, or guidance programs. If your child's school does not, you might want to discuss with her the three kinds of reading an adult has to master.

Three Kinds of Reading

When younger children read, they read in only one way. They have a single reading speed, usually 120 to 200 words per minute. They have a single approach to the text – to read all the words on the page and to get from them as much as possible. This reading works perfectly well eighty percent of the time, like a bike with only one gear. It's only going up hills or racing to destinations that requires a ten-speed derailleur. So, too, with reading.

Reading for Pleasure

Reading for pleasure is the way children read all the time and adults read most of the time. It's perfect for enjoying novels, the newspaper, and magazines. Every adult has a comfortable general reading speed. If you stop to measure, you'll likely find that you're reading this book a little more slowly than you would a novel, but your average speed will still run about 200 words per minute.

Reading speed tends to increase with education, from about 140 words per minute for a grade school grad to about 240 words per minute for a university graduate. So long as you read fast enough not to get bogged down (about 100 words per minute is enough for this) and not so fast that you have to work at it (say 700 words per minute, or 30 seconds a page), reading for pleasure feels comfortable.

The only problem with reading for pleasure is that it won't do some of the work that reading has to do in adult life. That's why teenagers need to learn two other kinds of reading.

Reading for Study

Reading for study is slow. It's laborious. It's a necessary drag. Your daughter can't read a biology textbook as fast as she reads a novel. Your son can't read the fine print on a credit card agreement as fast as he reads *Maclean's*. Reading for study involves different techniques and a different attitude.

An adult reader makes a decision to read for study. This is reading for work, for seeking information, for examining arguments and ideas. We apply this kind of reading to difficult material, whether it's the imagery of poetry, the ideas in a physics textbook, or the clauses in a contract. We do it with pencil in hand, a serious attitude in mind, and a sufficient amount of time set aside. Then we begin.

1. Overview. Look over the whole piece, get some sense of the structure and approach of the author, *then* go back and read a section at a time. It is sometimes very helpful to read the "about the author" section and the preface to understand the general slant of the book.

2. Slow down. Reading for study runs from twenty to eighty words per minute. If your eyes start travelling too quickly,

Tools Your Teen Can Do Without

Some items available to help teenagers in high school are of questionable value —

Encyclopaedia. Whether in print or CD ROM, an encyclopaedia rarely sees enough use to be worth $600 to $1,000. Far more sensible to use the sets at the library.

Thesaurus. While some English teachers swear by these, I've seen so many words misused because of "thesaurusitis" that I'd like to see them banned. Build your vocabulary by reading and using the dictionary, not by pulling words you've never read off a list.

Coloured Hi-lighters. Substitute colouring for thought. Far better to use a pencil to underline *and* comment in the margins. Then you can erase it all when the course is finished.

Their own phone line;
their own television set.
Parents who give teens their own phone lines or televisions, often for very "logical" reasons, are abdicating a key responsibility. The more private your teen becomes, the more isolated her life will be from yours. Stay connected.

start moving your lips as you read. Take the reading in small sections, then look away from the text and think: What is the author trying to get across? What is important in what I just read?

3. Reread. If you don't understand a sentence, go back and read it again. And again. Understanding is paramount; speed is trivial.

4. Read for details. The fine print and footnotes sometimes count more than the main text. That's where you'll learn that the research sample was too small or that department store credit card interest runs at a rate just shy of that of the local loan shark.

5. Take notes. Notes, comments, and responses scribbled into a notebook or in the margin ("Pavlov/bell/dog"; "Skinner is full of it") are far more valuable than simple underlining when reading for study. Marginal notes are a physical way to respond to the material – and responding encourages understanding. Underlining or highlighting merely produces a black and yellow page and the sense of having worked hard. Trade in your Hi-liters for pencils and respond to what you read.

6. Get help when you need it. Reading for study is sometimes done best with a dictionary beside you, or a calculator, or by calling for some advice on the phone. In casual reading, we can skip over difficult words or concepts, but not in reading for study.

Reading for Speed

Speed-reading is obviously the other extreme – where the reader skims rather than studies the material. Speed-reading involves both a change in reading rate and a change in attitude. There are certain methods a reader uses to make up for words and phrases missed in the push to get reading speed up towards 1,000 words a minute. Here are the basics:

1. Understand your own purpose. No one speed-reads for fun. You turn to speed-reading to find out something, or see if there's anything valuable in the books in front of you, or to check facts. A speed-reader always knows why she's reading and what she's looking for. Then she focuses her attention on exactly what she needs.

2. Orient yourself. A speed-reader always looks at the whole piece first to orient herself. Then she decides what portion to read and sets her reading speed depending on her own needs. Indexes and tables of contents save reading time by allowing you to go right to the relevent pages.

3. Use the big headings. Chapter titles and subheads show how the work is organized. They also tell the reader what sections can be skipped altogether and how fast other sections should be read. Read more slowly if the topic is close to what you need; speed up when it seems unrelated.

4. Keep up the pace. Reading for speed means pushing your eyes to handle 800 to 1,000 words per minute. Rumour has it that John F. Kennedy could skim-read at 20,000 words per minute, but Kennedy legends ranging from reading to sexual prowess are likely overstated. Still, any competent reader can double her reading speed with a little will-power and a fingertip.

5. Use a finger pointer. Running your finger down the page will keep your speed at a constant rate. You can buy machines to do the same thing, or cut a piece of cardboard

with a rectangle in the middle to focus your attention, but simply running your finger down a column of type – and keeping up with it – will have the same effect.

6. Take in more words at a glance. When you read, your eyes stop at several points along a line of type. Like this:

beginning/ readers/ stop/ at/ every/ word;
more sophisticated readers/ read in bunches or clusters/ of three to five words.

Each eye stop is called a fixation. The fewer fixations per line, the faster you'll read.

7. Avoid going backwards. When we read normally, our eyes "regress," or reread chunks of print that we didn't understand fully. Speed-reading advocates suggest that skipped words don't matter that much. Your brain will reconstruct what your eyes didn't quite see. By stopping eye regression, you can easily increase your reading speed by twenty-five percent or more.

By working on these techniques and practising on gradually more difficult material, many adults have managed to double their regular reading speed. Whether this is important to you depends on your school or your work, but every adult needs to learn to read for speed when required. Otherwise, we will spend some portions of our lives almost buried under print.

Building Critical Judgement

Teenagers are capable of wonderful flip-flops. They are incredibly enthusiastic one day – about Motley Crue, or Mrs. Jones the English teacher, or Leonard Cohen – and incredibly cynical the next – about Motley Crue, Mrs. Jones, and

Leonard Cohen. This mix of childish exuberance and growing sophistication is part of adolescent charm.

But we want more from our children than this. We know, as adults, that they will be called upon to make reasoned, critical judgements. They'll be voting, buying houses, looking for promotions at work, some day having children of their own – and all these require more judgement than enthusiasm.

That's what adult reading is all about. A book provides ideas and opinions that can and should be talked about. At home and at school, that talk should be promoted. Only through talk can your teenager understand some very important aspects of what she reads:

- Print carries the author's ideas – it is not holy writ.

- Authors can lie or misrepresent or be mistaken in print, just as in conversation.

- Authors have their own political and personal agendas, which must be respected or discounted in understanding what they write.

Small children have an inordinate respect for what they read. How many times have you heard, "But that's not what it says in the book, Mom!" For little kids, any book carries tremendous authority. The cynical attitude of many teenagers is a rebellion against that authority. This rebellion can reach such outrageous proportions as, "I don't believe anything I read."

What's needed in adolescence and adulthood is a critical stance, but not cynical abandonment. We want our children to understand that the *Globe and Mail* supports Conservative policy just as the Toronto *Star* promotes the Liberal cause. We want them to see that the current slew of articles about Madonna is part of a movie publicity package – and probably much less important to their lives than

What Are the Classics?

In the United States, former Secretary of Education William Bennett surveyed 325 journalists, teachers, and business leaders to come up with a list of the classics. Remembering that this list is quite American and includes only one woman writer, here's one try at the top twenty-five classics:

Shakespeare, *Macbeth, Hamlet*

The Bible

Mark Twain, *Huckleberry Finn*

Homer, *Odyssey, Iliad*

Charles Dickens, *Great Expectations*

Plato, *The Republic*

John Steinbeck, *The Grapes of Wrath*

William Hawthorne, *The Scarlet Letter*

Sophocles, *Oedipus*

Herman Melville, *Moby Dick*

George Orwell, *1984*

H.D. Thoreau, *Walden*

Robert Frost, poems

Walt Whitman, *Leaves of Grass*

F. Scott Fitzgerald, *The Great Gatsby*

Chaucer, *The Canterbury Tales*

Karl Marx, *Communist Manifesto*

Aristotle, *Poetics*

Emily Dickinson, poems

Fyodr Dostoevsky, *Crime and Punishment*

William Faulkner, *The Sound and the Fury*

J.D. Salinger, *The Catcher in the Rye*

A. De Tocqueville, *Democracy in America*

Jane Austen, *Pride and Prejudice*

Emerson: essays

our tedious, but essential, constitutional debates.

And we want all this at the same time as our children are least interested in what we, their parents, have to say.

So make demands of your child's high school. If everything you see from your son's history course or your daughter's English course seems to be short answer or multiple-choice, talk to the teachers and the principal. According to Jean Piaget, the Swiss psychologist, and other researchers, our children can't fully reason until the age of thirteen or fourteen. That gives our high schools only four or five years to develop children's sophisticated reasoning skills. Multiple-choice tests and simple factual recall questions won't build the skills your children need.

Demand more. High school students should be reading intensively at school and widely at home – as part of the program. High school programs should be calling for research, argument, debate, and a great deal of writing to match all the reading. And teachers in the school should always challenge your children, regardless of their abilities, to stretch themselves intellectually.

Then be sure to follow through at home. Teenagers don't have to be questioned about their every sentence, but they can be asked to explain or defend their ideas. The correct response to "This book is stupid" isn't "Shut up and read it anyway"; it's "Why do you think so?" The correct response to "I don't understand this dumb history assignment" isn't "Go back and try it again"; it's "What do you think the author might be trying to say?" If you're there at the kitchen table with your teen, the talk can begin. You've reached a point in your child's school life where you certainly won't have all the answers, but you'll know far better what the questions should be.

What Teenagers Do Read

Teenagers who do read read unpredictably. A grade thirteen student of mine last year brought in her own books to read when she had a spare period. One week I made some notes on Alison's reading: a Constance Beresford-Howe novel on Monday, a handful of Robert Munsch picture books on Tuesday, Kahlil Gibran on Wednesday, *Cosmopolitan* on Thursday, and back to the Beresford-Howe novel on Friday. This same girl tried to convince me to put *Alice in Wonderland* on the teen "must-have" list because she'd found so much in it the second time through.

Alison, like most teenagers, is not the finished person she would like to think she is. Teenagers are still being formed – or forming themselves. They haven't let go of their own childhood, yet they are busy exploring the adult world and trying to find their place in it. As a result, avid teen readers are looking for information everywhere: novels, poetry, letters, philosophy, religion, biography and history.

For your teenager, there are types of books that serve as a transition from children's fiction to adult literature. Some of these may keep your child reading right through the grade nine slump until she's ready to handle adult books.

- Realistic young adult fiction. Walk into any library and you'll see the rack: paperback novels, about 175 pages long, with teenage central characters confronting – and usually triumphing over – problems ranging from divorce to date rape. The pioneers in this field – Paul Zindel, S.E. Hinton, Robert Cormier, Kevin Major, John Craig – sought to give young people a literature that valued teenage experience and didn't shy away from the real difficulties kids face. This genre remains important, especially for teens up to age fourteen or fifteen.

- Fantasy. Fantasy is a mixture of the classic adventure novel and some Sir Walter Scott derring-do with the long saga of

The Quirky List

Older teenage readers frequently show bizarre tastes – just as adult readers do. With cautions that the language is frequently foul, here are some hot items for the grade eleven/twelve set:

William Burroughs, *Junky* (Penguin, 1977). A vile novel by the author of *Naked Lunch* (Grove, 1959). For the druggy, life-is-meaningless crowd.

Herman Hesse, *Siddhartha* (Bantam, 1922) and his better book *Demian* (Bantam, 1919). Both appeal to older teens busy looking for themselves.

Franz Kafka, *Metamorphosis* (Bantam, 1946) has a kind of cult following in the high schools, augmented by the movie on the author's life.

Jack Kerouac, *On the Road* (Penguin, 1957), and Allen Ginsberg, *Howl* (City Lights, 1959) are for adolescents looking at 1950s-style rebellion to see how it was done in the old days. Ken Kesey, *One Flew Over the Cuckoo's Nest* (Penguin, 1962) also appeals to some.

George Orwell, *1984* (Penguin, 1949), and Aldous Huxley, *Brave New World* (Harper-Collins, 1932) appeal to teens who are convinced we're all going to hell in a handbasket.

Daniel Richler, *Kicking Tomorrow* (McClelland & Stewart, 1991) is the foulest coming-of-age novel I've ever read, but with surprisingly conservative values underneath. A far cry from his father's *Duddy Kravitz*.

What Rock Musicians Read

Here's a much-condensed version of a CITY-TV/THE NEW MUSIC listing. Try this on your teenager:

- Bryan Adams:
  Emily Carr, *The Book of Small* (Stoddart, 1942).

- Rick Astley:
  Martin Amis, *Success, The Rachel Papers* (Penguin 1978, 1973).

- Barney Bentall:
  Thomas Hardy, *The Mayor of Casterbridge* (Penguin, 1886).
  John Irving, *Hotel New Hampshire* (Dell, 1981).

- Duran Duran (as a group):
  Truman Capote, *In Cold Blood* (Signet, 1965).
  Clive Barker, *Weaveworld* (HarperCollins, 1987).
  Mervyn Peake, *Titus Groan* (Methuen, 1968).

- Gowan:
  Herman Hesse, *Siddhartha* and *Steppenwolf* (Bantam, 1922, 1928).

- Deborah Harry:
  Peter Straub, *Ghost Story* (Cape, 1979).
  Hubert Selby, *Last Exit to Brooklyn* (Grove, 1964).

Arthurian legend, set in some indeterminate time where magic and heroic deeds somehow seem plausible. Once lumped in with science-fiction, fantasy has now become its own genre, with writers ranging from Lloyd Alexander and Madeleine L'Engle for the younger set to Piers Anthony and Ursula Le Guin for the more mature teenager.

- Science-fiction. These days, fantasy is pushing sci-fi books off the bookstore shelves, but this genre remains popular with many teenagers, especially boys. Again, these books offer heroism, philosophy, adventure, and a simplified moral universe that is empowering reading for young people.

- Romance. With effective marketing of junior Harlequins like "The Twins" and "The Babysitters' Club," teenage girls are moving on naturally to real Harlequins, Silhouettes, and spicier cousins like Harlequin Mystique. Teen readers ignore the interchangeable characters and plots to get lost in the idealized romance they hope to find later in real life. More sophisticated readers will find books by Barbara Cartland and Danielle Steel form a crossover to mysteries and popular fiction. The growing field of historical romance offers idealized characters and plots in novels with solid historical settings.

- Horror. The rise of horror seemed to follow the decline of the western as a genre – and this may say something quite terrible about the current direction of our society. Nonetheless, Stephen King is probably the single most popular author among adolescents, and his creepy novels are likely to be a cut above the positively gory films your son or daughter might otherwise be watching. Testing out their capacity for fear through the books of King, Christopher Pike (for the younger set), and Peter Straub (for the brighter readers) is as much a part of adolescence as testing out the capacity for dreaming through romance fiction.

- Classics. There are still teenagers who enjoy reading great works of literature, especially if this taste is quietly encouraged at home and at school. Some older teens spend several months reading "The Russians" (usually Dostoevsky more than Tolstoy or Gogol), or Franz Kafka, or Jean-Paul Sartre, or F. Scott Fitzgerald, or Margaret Laurence. Some will read classic horror writers like H.P. Lovecraft, or classic sci-fi like Ray Bradbury. Others will get excited about a particular writer's work if there's a current movie or a fad at school to spur motivation.

- Non-fiction. A fair number of teenagers will read only biographies of rock stars, or books on automobile racing, or magazine after magazine on computers. Chapter 10 goes into more detail on reading tied to particular interests.

- And all the rest. Some teenagers read more widely and with greater sophistication than their parents. If that is true in your family, or you've fallen out of the habit of reading for pleasure, the next chapter is for you.

- Jon Bon Jovi:
  Charles Bukowski, *Hollywood: A Novel* (Black Sparrow, 1989).

- M.C. Hammer:
  The Bible.

- Kris Kristofferson:
  Joseph Heller, *Catch 22* (Dell, 1961).

- Simon Le Bon of Duran Duran:
  Gabriel Garcia Marquez, *One Hundred Years of Solitude* (Harper-Collins, 1970).
  Hunter S. Thompson, *Fear and Loathing in Las Vegas* (Warner, 1971).

- Jane Siberry:
  Agatha Christie murder mysteries.

- Paul Stanley of Kiss:
  Kurt Vonnegut, *Breakfast of Champions* (Dell, 1973).
  Ayn Rand, *Atlas Shrugged* (Signet/NAL, 1957).

- Sting:
  Robert Bly, *Iron John* (Addison Wesley, 1990).
  Anne Rice, *The Vampire Chronicles* (Ballantine, 1985, etc.).

- Suzanne Vega:
  Simone de Beauvoir, *The Second Sex* (Vintage, 1957).

Some Good Bets for Your Teen's Bookshelf

A caution: by this age, your child's interests and tastes may be so specific that purchasing books on other subjects might be met with grunts or sneers. But if you don't broaden your teen's reading, who will? Here's a twelve-book starter list:

Douglas Adams, *A Hitchhiker's Guide to the Galaxy* (Pan, 1979). Monty Python meets science-fiction; based on the radio series but very well written. Strong appeal for bright teens.

V.C. Andrews, *Flowers In the Attic* (Pocket Books, 1979) and other titles. These are low-rent, family-terror titles, but awesomely popular with girls from grades seven to nine.

Robert Cormier, *The Chocolate War* (Dell, 1974). This author's most famous book is about terror in a New England private school. His more recent novel *The Bumblebee Flies Anyway* (Dell, 1983), moved me to tears.

William Golding, *Lord of the Flies* (Faber, 1954) wasn't written for teenagers, but it has become popular with them. Death and savagery on a deserted island. A grade eleven standard.

Marilyn Halvorson, *Cowboys Don't Cry* (Stoddart, 1984) for good readers; *Bull Rider* (Macmillan, 1989) for weak readers. Two novels about families, rodeos, and ranching in the Canadian west.

S.E. Hinton, *The Outsiders* (Dell, 1967). Written when the author was just seventeen, this novel provides a picture of gang conflict about as accurate as that in *West Side Story*. Nonetheless, young teens love it.

Stephen King, *The Dead Zone* (Signet, 1979). How can any kid grow up without reading at least one Stephen King chiller? This one is less gruesome than others.

Kevin Major, *Dear Bruce Springsteen* (Dell, 1987). Major's most accessible novel – a touching picture of loneliness and teenage angst. If this clicks, try the author's first novel, *Far From Shore* (Dell, 1978).

Harry Mazer, *Snow Bound* (Dell, 1973). Adventure and self-realization in a snowstorm, for readers age eleven and up. Mazer is one of the top American young-adult writers and this book shows all his skill.

J.D. Salinger, *The Catcher in the Rye* (Bantam, 1951). A classic coming-of-age novel that still appeals to bright teens. Attempts to ban this now-innocuous book just add to its appeal.

Paul Zindel, *The Pigman* (Dell, 1968) and others. Zindel won a Pulitzer prize for his play *The Effect of Gamma Rays on Man-in-the-Moon Marigolds* but he's won the hearts of millions of teens with his young adult novels. Realistic and poignant.

CHAPTER 9

The Adult Reader

Throughout this book, I've been looking at reading as a lifelong process, as something we learn and develop from infancy through school and into adulthood. It would be foolish, then, to suggest that learning to read is somehow complete by the end of high school or university. It's not. As adults, we continue to learn to read in ways that can enrich both our appreciation of books and our own lives.

The tremendous advantage we have as adult readers is experience. I remember as a child trying to tackle some of the great works of literature with the intellectual tools I had available at the time. In grade six, a number of us decided to read *Macbeth* out loud because somebody had said it was an important play. So at age eleven, my friends Irwin, Marshall, Robbie, Anita, and I read the words in *Macbeth* with all the dramatic passion we could muster. When we finally finished the play, none of us could understand what all the fuss was about. How could this play have survived for 350 years and be so revered by all these adults? For us, it was just a bunch of weird, old-fashioned words with a story about a greedy man, his crazy wife, and the good guys

What Do We Read?

The people who responded to the *Reading in Canada 1991* survey are a fairly literate group. They claimed to have read twenty-four books in the past year, five of them by Canadian authors. Here's a breakdown by type of book:

Mysteries: 4.2 books

Romance: 4.2

Other fiction: 3.1

Self-help and how-to books: 2.6

Other non-fiction: 2.5

Science-fiction: 2.3

History, current events: 1.7

Classic literature: 1.5

Biography: 1.2

Cartoon books: 1.1

Poetry: 0.3

winning at the end. Quite simply, we didn't get it.

I didn't tackle *Macbeth* again until grade eleven, with another five years of worldly experience under my belt. This time I "got" a little more of it. Using my sketchy knowledge of Freudian psychology, I decided the play was really about sexual frustration. The fact that my own life was largely about sexual frustration was impossible to admit at the time, but I could certainly see the problem writ large in Shakespeare. As an adolescent, I managed to get my first handle on the play, but it was only a beginning.

I came back to *Macbeth* again as a teacher. At age thirty-four, I had a bit more under my belt: another seventeen years of living, two children growing up, experience producing and directing two school musicals. Unlike my grade eleven students, I was no longer interested in the sexual problems of the Macbeths. The scene that riveted me was the one in which Macduff is told of the death of his children. That scene literally brought tears to my eyes.

Nor will I pretend that my readings of *Macbeth* are complete these days, in my forties, as I see aspects of politics that I'd never noticed before. What will my reading of *Macbeth* find when I am fifty or sixty or seventy? I suspect it will be characters and themes I can't begin to uncover at this stage in my life.

Does this mean that I am a *better* reader now than I was at age fifteen or twenty-five or thirty-five? Probably not. I am a different reader than I was, reaching out to the book or the play in a different way.

So our children must keep reading great literature in high school, and we must keep reaching back to that literature as adults. Again and again in my adult life, I come back to words that I read in high school and university but only dimly understood: lines of poetry from Thomas Hardy, John Donne and T.S. Eliot, speeches from Shakespeare and George Bernard Shaw, and Arthur Miller's *Death of a Salesman*, chunks of prose from Joseph Conrad or Charles Dickens or Dostoevsky. I find in these bits and pieces the solace I need at a given moment, the wisdom I need to understand or move forward. I am a member of a generation that was inundated by the popular – from early television to the Beatles – but the words that have stood by me are those that have already passed a more substantial test of time. Sometimes I look at our young people, headphones plugged into their ears, Metallica or Madonna plugged into their minds, and I can only hope that they are finding a way to get something more substantial upon which to build a life.

The Resonance of Words

In the first chapters of this book, I described the ways that young children get beyond print to the dream or ideas of a book. As adults, I think we use books in an additional way – to get beyond print to words and images that bring a delicious resonance.

A book or story that is meaningful for adults resonates within, it touches something in our bones. A passage can make us respond with "I've thought that," or "I've felt that." Print connects our humanity at its deepest level with the ideas, hopes, and dreams of another.

Read with me:

It is a winter's night in 1936 in Halifax, Nova Scotia. A small boy is being read to. He is warm from a hot bath, wearing striped flannel pyjamas and a thick woollen dressing gown with a tasselled cord. He has dropped off his slippers to slide his bare feet between the cushions of the sofa.

Outside, a salty wind blows snow against the panes of the windows. It sifts under the front door and through the three ventilation holes in the storm windows, creating tiny drifts. Foghorns are grumping far in

"If you read a story that really involves you, your body will tell you that you are living through the experience. You will recognize feelings that have physical signs – increased heart rate, sweaty palms, or calm, relaxed breathing and so on, depending on your mood. These affects are the same you would feel in similar real-life experiences – fear, anger, interest, joy, shame or sadness. Amazingly, you can actually 'live' experience without moving anything but your eyes across a page."
– From Joseph Gold, *Read for Your Life* (Fitzhenry and Whiteside, 1990).

the distance. The coal fire in the basket grate burns intense and silent. His mother reads . . . .

So Robert MacNeil transports us in the opening paragraphs of *Wordstruck*. I am moved by the sheer beauty of the writing: the foghorns grumping, the tasselled cord on the boy's dressing gown, the repeated *s* sounds in the salty wind words of the second paragraph. And I resonate with the images MacNeil provides. I grew up inland, but I've since felt the salty wind of Halifax. It was my father, not my mother, who read to me in my crumpled pyjamas, but I know that memory – that feeling – and it is part of my response to MacNeil's printed words. Other details, too, are rich for me in remembrance: those old storm windows with the three ventilation holes where my friends and I would run telephone wires, or whisper conversations when they weren't allowed in the house. The feeling of a hot bath and the tingling of the skin when I emerged, warmed despite the chill room. These images from my own life are conjured up as I read MacNeil's prose.

As adults, we can savour the words, the images, and our own memories. We automatically slow down our reading when we come to a section that especially grips us just to relish the prose. While we may zip through a description of Halifax harbour at 400 words per minute or more, we will slow down our reading to less than half that speed to enjoy the words that resonate within us. When we read, unlike the experience of television, we have control over the images that are presented to us. This control gives us the power to linger over the words and to enjoy the images and memories they create in our minds.

All-Time Best Mysteries

According to a reader survey at the Sleuth of Baker Street bookstore in Toronto, these are the best mysteries ever . . .

1. Josephine Tey, *The Daughter of Time* (Penguin, 1951).

2. Arthur Conan Doyle, *The Hound of the Baskervilles* (Penguin, 1902).

3. Dorothy Sayers, *Gaudy Night* (Coronet, 1935).

4. Raymond Chandler, *The Big Sleep* (Vintage, 1939).

5. Dorothy Sayers, *Nine Tailors* (Coronet, 1934).

6. Dashiell Hammett, *The Maltese Falcon* (Vintage, 1929).

7. P.D. James, *A Taste for Death* (Penguin, 1986).

8. Agatha Christie, *Murder on the Orient Express* (Pocket, 1934).

9. Elizabeth George, *A Great Deliverance* (Bantam, 1988).

Finding Time

The joys of adult reading are available to us only if we make the time to read. Simply finding quiet time is becoming more and more difficult as our leisure hours shrink. According to one measure, the number of free hours available to North Americans peaked in 1973 at twenty-six hours a week and has shrunk by a third since then. Simultaneously, the demands placed on our leisure – by everything from television to sports to dining out – have multiplied. The result is obvious: we read less.

And we read differently. Witold Rybczynski in his brilliant book *Waiting for the Weekend* talks about the way reading has changed as our leisure time shrinks and fragments. To read a novel, for instance, we should devote a certain amount of time every day. We cannot begin Timothy Findley's *The Telling of Lies* on Sunday morning, put the book down for a week, and hope to pick up where we left off. A big novel has too many characters, too many plots and subplots, too many themes for our memory to hold that long.

Maybe that is the reason we've seen such an increase in short literary forms: the short story collection, the formula novel, the magazine article. Reading a short story, for instance, is a complete experience that takes the twenty minutes most of us have before bed. Many mass-produced novels like Harlequin romances are only 50,000 words long and can be completed with about three hours of reading. Magazines require even less. The breakthrough of *People* magazine a few years ago wasn't based on great design or new material. It was based on very short articles. Now there's hardly a magazine on the racks that doesn't have several sections or columns that used to be called "'snippets," tiny, 200-word fragments that compress stories into snappy prose that grabs our attention, but not our time. Even the venerable *Harper's*, an intellectual magazine for 143 years, has a "Readings" section for short articles which takes up a third of the magazine.

This kind of reading simply isn't enough. In order to enter fully into the story, to feel with the

How do Adults Pick Books

According to the *Reading in Canada 1991* survey results, we choose books many different ways. Here's what readers mentioned when asked how they became aware of the book they were currently reading, in order:

1. through conversation with friends, family;

2. interested in author;

3. browsing or display in bookstore;

4. browsing or display in library;

5. book club promotion;

6. read a book review or article;

7. saw it as a movie or TV show;

8. heard about it on radio or TV;

9. saw newspaper or magazine advertising.

Best Books to Take to the Cottage

Compiled by the staff of *Cottage Life* magazine:

1. Gabriel Garcia Marquez, *One Hundred Years of Solitude* (HarperCollins, 1970). A dazzling, magical family saga. Cottage Country will fade away and you'll feel yourself swallowed up in lush, steamy South American heat.

2. John Irving, *A Prayer for Owen Meany* (Lester & Orpen Dennys, 1989) or any of Irving's wonderfully rich novels. We have a special fondness for the funny-voiced Owen Meany WHO TALKS LIKE THIS.

3. J.R.R. Tolkien, *The Lord of the Rings* (Unwin, 1954). Heroic deeds, mythical language, and down-to-earth humour. Ideal read-aloud stuff.

4. Colleen McCullough, *The Thorn Birds* (Futura, 1980). A heck of a good story – and full of interesting bits about life in nineteenth- and twentieth-century Australia.

5. Howard Engel, *Murder Sees the Light* (Viking, 1984). All the Benny Cooperman mysteries are fun, but this one has an added bonus for cottagers: it's set in Algonquin Park.

Runners up: **6.** Bill Bryson, *Neither Here Nor There* (Secker & Warburg, 1991). **7.** James West Davidson and John Rugge, *Great Heart* (Viking, 1988). **8.** Tim Cahill, *Jaguars Ripped My Flesh* (Bantam, 1987). **9.** Umberto Eco, *The Name of the Rose* (Warner, 1983). **10.** Elmore Leonard, *Get Shorty* (Dell, 1990).

characters, to join the imaginative world of the author, we must give a book time. A big novel, like John Irving's *A Prayer for Owen Meany*, will have over 300,000 words in its 430 pages and require some eighteen hours to complete. In the book trade, this is considered a summer book because that's when people head off to cottages and the beach, apparently with enough time to read it. Certainly reading a big novel on vacation is a joy, but why should that be the only time for it?

We find more than twenty-three hours a week to watch television. We have found an additional nine hours to add to our work week since the 1950s. We regularly find four hours a week to travel to and from work. Surely there is time in our lives to read more and to read with greater regularity. But we must be aggressive to seize that time:

- After reading with your child, take the rest of that hour to read for yourself.

- At breakfast, or just before leaving for work, set aside fifteen minutes for reading a book with your coffee.

- Make reading time a special time. As one person suggested to me, "The children aren't allowed to bother me so long as I'm reading – at least, not until I turn a page."

- Set aside a reading time on Sunday afternoon. I have a friend who manages to watch football on TV with the sound off, play Mozart on the stereo, *and* read a novel. He maintains that in this way he combines all the joys of life at one sitting.

- Transform some TV time into reading time. There might well be half an hour between dinner and the 9:00 TV movie for a good read.

- Organize a time for reading as you might organize a time for daily exercise. I love to open a book at 5:00 PM, sitting on the deck, knowing I have half an hour before I have to worry about dinner.

Remember that reading was first – and should still be – a social experience. Nothing will get a person as excited about a book as a strong recommendation from someone else. A book you read and enjoyed should be lent out and talked about. Part of the joy of reading is in sharing – "Have you come to the part where . . .?" "Isn't it great when . . .?" I was so excited by *Waiting for the Weekend* that I spent most of a dinner party talking about it, then I lent it to a friend, then spent another dinner talking to him about it. The thriller *The Silence of the Lambs* by Thomas Harris may not be great literature, but it's been read by everyone in my family because enthusiasm for a good read is contagious. Perhaps you can join a group of friends to exchange book enthusiasms – and exchange books as well. Some libraries and communities even have semi-formal reading groups where the members read a chosen novel each month and then discuss the book and its ideas. These groups are both excellent ways to spur your own reading.

Reading is too important to be left for a few weeks of vacation, or the Christmas holidays, or limited to the daily newspaper and *Maclean's*. We must give ourselves time – serious, quiet time – to read and respond to books. A reader for life, by definition, finds time to fit reading into an adult day.

Reading for Our Greater Uses

Too much adult reading today is purely practical. In our work lives we plough through papers, manuals, memos, directives, and tax forms so

A Reading Group

There's nothing like a strong recommendation from a friend to get you reading a book. Reading groups pull together a number of friends who share their responses to the books they've read, lend books to each other, and otherwise restore the social context to reading. Sometimes these are organized through public libraries, but all that's really needed to get one going is an organizer and a coffee pot.

A reading salon is a little more focused. Frequently, the talk at a salon will centre on a single book or a single topic. Sometimes there's a leader to get discussion going. The magazine *Utne Reader* offers suggestions and addresses of people in your area who would be interested in being part of a salon. Write to:

Neighborhood Salon Association,
1624 Harmon Place
Minneapolis, Minnesota 55403.

that the act of reading itself can be reduced to the most mundane of uses. Even in our reading for pleasure, the "information piece" and the practical book on shed construction are usurping more of our time and our money. Yet books can serve much greater uses if we could admit to more important needs.

The decline and seeming irrelevance of poetry in our time is a good case in point. For thousands of years, poetry was the vehicle that carried the wisdom and consummate artistry of the writer. It was the form of expression of Virgil, Shakespeare, and John Keats. It was the genre that merited the highest expectations when novels were merely popular entertainment and short stories just bedtime reading.

But poetry today gets little or no attention. You'll find precious little poetry on your bookstore shelves and only a fraction of that written by living poets about the world around us. Yet poetry has a capacity to illuminate our lives – especially our adult lives – in ways that no other genre can. In its compression, its concentration on idea and gesture, its formal discipline whether rhymed or unrhymed, poetry is "of use" to adults. We should be reading Adrienne Rich, Robert Bly, Paul Dutton, and Ted Hughes for what they see and what we can, as adults, see with them.

Yet poetry is in decline. It is almost as if we have allowed adult life to be side-tracked into the merely practical, or our problems trivialized into thirty-minute television shows complete with laugh track.

Joseph Gold, in his wonderful book, *Read For Your Life*, talks about the ways books can open up worlds of emotion and remembrance for adult readers. Gold feels that fiction, especially, has the power to help us deal psychologically with the problems of adult life – marriage, divorce, death, humiliation, disappointment, aging, rejection. Gold writes, "Literature speaks for us, says

Some Contemporary Poets Worth Reading

George Swede, one of Canada's most accessible poets himself, selected these "contemporary, charismatic, and Canadian poets" for adults who want to start reading poetry again.

Jeanette Armstrong: a native Canadian who makes the spirit of her people soar again.

George Elliott Clarke: an African-Canadian poet who speaks to us in a language that echoes blues and rap.

Lorna Crozier: a Saskatoon poet who evokes a gamut of emotions about practically everything under the Prairie skies.

David Donnell: a sensuous and humorous chronicler of the times in and around Toronto.

Don McKay: an Ontario poet who writes captivatingly about nature. Perfect for reading at the cottage.

Erin Mouré: a Prairie-born, Montreal-based feminist whose work even macho males will enjoy.

back to us truths too painful for us to utter in our own words."

Books provide an analogue to real life, a model that allows us to experience other lives, other thoughts, and other emotions. Reading is the skill that allows books to be used in this way. For ourselves, as adults, just as much as for our children, we have to make time for it in our lives.

CHAPTER 10

Exciting the Bored Reader

It can happen to the nicest kids. Your son Jonah, a good enough reader through grade five, suddenly declares that reading is boring. When you offer to read a book with him, the response written on his face says, "Do I have to?" Or your daughter Jennifer, who brought home piles of books right through middle school, is now reading only one novel a month in grade eight, and that's just because a book report is due for her English teacher. When you offer to read with Jennifer in the evening, she gives you that withering almost-adolescent look and declares, "Mom, I *know* how to read."

Both Jennifer and Jonah do know how to read. All the technical skills are there: the sight vocabulary and instant phonic analysis and reasonable reading speed. They would score just fine on any standardized reading test. But neither of the kids is reading, and that's ultimately going to hurt them. One American researcher has declared that unless children and adults read twenty-two minutes a day, their reading skills will go into decline. I'm sceptical about magic numbers like "twenty-two minutes a day," but I do know that kids who stop reading start to fall behind their

143

Martyn Godfrey's Six Sure-Fire Books for Bored Middle School Readers

Martyn Godfrey, one of Canada's most popular writers for the middle school crowd, picks these six titles for the kids who don't want to read anything:

1. Frank O'Keeffe, *Guppy Love* (KidsCan, 1986). "A funny, funny story that had me laughing out loud. Natalie and Janet are two of the most delightful characters ever created."

2. Lyle Weis, *No Problem, We'll Fix It* (General, 1991). "A city-kid-visits-the-farm novel which is fresh and different. A hilarious bathroom scene makes this an unforgettable read."

3. Gordon Korman, *MacDonald Hall Goes Hollywood* (Scholastic, 1991). "I'm a great fan of all Gordon's novels, especially the Bruno and Boots series. They never get any funnier than this story."

4. John Ibbitson, *The Wimp and the Jock* (Maxwell Macmillan, 1986). "Randy the wimp stumbles through football tryouts. So fast-paced I read the novel in one sitting."

5. S.E. Hinton, *Rumble Fish* (Dell, 1975). "Rusty James is an irresistible character in this more serious novel."

6. Sylvia McNicoll, *More Than Money* (Nelson, 1988). "Braces, boys, and babysitting. Fast and witty."

classmates. They lose ground in vocabulary, in comprehension, in advanced thinking skills, even in the ability to write. If Jennifer and Jonah stay stalled with the skills of their grade level, they'll be significantly behind many of their peers in two years' time – and in real trouble within four years.

I'm using Jennifer and Jonah as examples of "bored readers," kids who are not illiterate but aliterate. Jennifer and Jonah have the skills, but they are developing an indifference to print. Unlike the reluctant readers I'll discuss in Chapter 11, Jennifer and Jonah have no intellectual or medical problems to explain their reading attitude. They are not among that five to ten percent of the school population with reading difficulties that require testing, analysis, and remediation. Jennifer and Jonah are just bored with books.

In Jennifer's case, we have a young adolescent whose life is suddenly taken over by the prospect of boys, the secrets and rumours that run through junior high school, an emotional life that seems to take all her energy and the growing demands of the school curriculum. Compared to the real life she's discovering, Jennifer finds kids' books too tame and teenage novels too safe. She could probably read adult pot-boilers, but her school library doesn't have any, her junior library card won't let her check them out, and her parents wouldn't approve anyway. So she reads only what she has to for school, borrows the occasional book from a friend without telling her parents, and spends many hours plopped in front of the TV or with the stereo blaring in her bedroom or booming through headphones. Jennifer will likely start reading again some years after this phase, which educator David Booth calls the teenage "fallow period." But in the meantime her reading and intellectual skills will be stagnant.

Jonah's case is more serious because his boredom will hold back progress in reading at a more crucial stage. While Jennifer's grade eight reading skills are probably sufficient for her to function right through high school, Jonah's grade five skills will doom him, unless they improve, to semi-literacy. He'll end up at the bottom stream in high school, and eventually he'll be stuck in an adult life without books – unless something is done quickly.

Get Involved, Again

For many bored readers, the solution is quite simple – renewed involvement by parents using the three Rs. Parents must renew a commitment to read with their child every day, even if it starts out simply with books assigned by the school. Parents must reach into their wallets for money to provide books or magazines for their child, perhaps augmented with a bi-weekly library trip made together. And parents must make sure there's time for reading to happen, by turning off the TV, or cutting back the ballet lessons, or putting limits on time on the phone. Routines must change.

The problem with this simple prescription is that routines are very hard to change. Your kids will resist your involvement, seeing it as an intrusion; they'll call your offer to buy books a bribe; they'll say that any new rules around the house are "unfair," or "fascist," or worse.

Make the changes anyway.

I'm not one to call for raw displays of parental power, but there's much to be said for parental *resolve*. The reasons behind the changes should be presented seriously, and the changes should be enforced despite initial whining and complaints. Often school provides a good excuse for initiating change. One opening: "Your dad and I were talking to your teacher last week, and she's concerned that you're not reading as much as you used to . . ." Another approach is to use this book: "Your mom and I have been reading a book lately about the importance of reading.

Those "Series" Books

There's a mixed opinion in the book business about books that come out in a series, like Sweet Valley High, as opposed to individual titles issued in "trade." The Children's Bookstore in Toronto and many libraries won't even put series books on the shelves. On the other hand, many chain bookstores have so many series books that there's no room left for trade novels.

There's probably a middle ground that would give kids a chance at Sweet Valley High books without cutting into sales of Jean Little's *Little by Little* or Martha Brook's *Paradise Cafe*. And there are probably some series books that might turn on a bored reader because the concept is so much like TV. Turn to the next page for my picks.

Best of the Series

Degrassi Junior High and Kids of Degrassi Street (Lorimer). Yes, they're TV spin-offs, but they also tackle real problems like alcoholism, teenage sex, and drugs.

Series Canada and Series 2000 (Maxwell Macmillan) are really for kids who have trouble reading, but some titles like *Ice Hawk* and *Wild Night* would stand up against any trade novel.

Flare series (Avon). If your child wants something like Harlequin Romances, at least the books should be well done. Try this series.

Steve Jackson and Ian Livinston's Fighting Fantasy series (Penguin). These are fantasy books that kids "play" while they read, skipping from section to section to create many different plots. Much like the action-oriented *Choose Your Own Adventure* (Bantam) novels.

We've both become concerned that you don't read as much as you used to, and we're afraid that it's going to hurt you in the long run. So we've decided to change one or two things around here . . . " A third approach is to talk about your child's welfare: "You know that reading is important, maybe the most important thing that's worked on in school. We've decided to promote it a little more at home, starting tomorrow . . ."

Then keep to your new routines. If the new rules call for a quiet time between seven and eight, don't make yourselves an exception. Leave the dishes in the sink, take the phone off the hook, disconnect the TV, take the batteries out of the Walkman – and read. If the new rules say you'll read together at 9:00 PM, then do it exactly at 9:00 until the routine gets established. If the new rules say there'll be a bookstore trip once a month, start right away, telling your son he can choose one book on his own and that you're going to choose one more from the suggestions in this book.

It is, quite literally, never too late to help the bored reader. One of the consultants for this book tells the story of a Toronto teacher who inadvertently ended up helping his son stop being a bored reader. The father, a senior elementary science teacher, kept challenging his son's middle school to do a better job spurring his son's reading – test more, challenge more, require more, do more to make the child a better reader. None of this was successful, and the son's reading remained sporadic and forced.

In 1987, the Toronto elementary teachers went on strike, and father and son were stuck at home, bored. The father decided that his own son's education wouldn't be sacrificed, and he started bringing home books from the library and bookstore, two a day. He and his son read the books, sometimes together, sometimes separately and spent time talking about them. When the strike was over a month later, the son had a changed attitude towards reading and books, and had become a much more competent reader.

The father, of course, is still convinced that his child's school wasn't doing its job. But the truth is that the father wasn't doing his job until the strike spurred him to do so. Suddenly the son was given quiet time, an interested parent, and a chance to talk about what he read – and he became a reader. Inadvertently, the father was following the three Rs, and the results speak for themselves.

Plug into Interests

While some of us will read anything that passes in front of our eyes, from cereal boxes to medical textbooks, the bored reader is much pickier. The bored reader will not look at the newspaper just because it's on the kitchen table, or pick up a magazine in the bathroom just because there's time, or begin a novel unless there's some reason to do so. The bored reader is choosy. The bored reader wants reading that ties into his interests. And the bored reader needs a push.

If you've been reading with your child every day, you already know what he likes and dislikes in terms of reading. But if you haven't been doing this, you will have to go back and rediscover your child's interests. As parents, we are often too close or too far way from our own children. We are too close when we know our children's favourite breakfast cereal, but never hear about their dreams or fears or what makes them cry at night. We are too far when we lecture them about coming in after 1:00AM when they're really worried about birth control, AIDS, and the stories their ex-boyfriends might or might not be telling around school. If your child is a bored reader, you'll have to take a middle position to find books which will appeal.

Let's start with four questions:

- What are three things your child is interested in?

Six Great Sports Books

Lesley Choyce, *Skateboard Shakedown* (Formac, 1989). The skateboard action in this novel for middle schoolers never stops.

Martyn Godfrey, *Baseball Crazy* (Lorimer, 1987). For Blue Jay fans, this novel follows the action to Florida.

Howard Liss, *The Giant Book of Strange But True Sports Stories* (Random House, 1976). Breezy, fascinating, and the stories are real!

Marilyn Halvorson, *Bull Rider* (Maxwell Macmillan, 1989). Probably the best easy-to-read sports book ever.

Brian McFarlane, *Hockey: the Book for Kids* (KidsCan, 1990). Solid, oversized non-fiction, with illustrations.

Scott Young, *Scrubs on Skates* (McClelland & Stewart), 1952. A great hockey story, now in an attractive paperback.

- What three activities are your child and his friends involved in?

- What three adult activities would your child like to do someday?

- What were the last three books/stories/magazines that your child seemed to enjoy?

Christopher Pyke: Stephen King for Middle Schoolers

Matching the current popularity of horror movies, writer Christopher Pyke offers a great scary read for the grade six and up crowd. Try *Slumber Party* (Scholastic, 1985), *Weekend* (Scholastic, 1986), *Scavenger Hunt* (Archway, 1989), and *Die Softly* (Archway, 1991).

If your child gets hooked on Christopher Pyke, try some horror books by Caroline Cooney (Scholastic Point) or the much better-written suspense novels by Lois Duncan (Dell).

If you can already answer all four questions, you have a dozen bits of information with which to select books from the library or the bookstore. But if you're like most parents, the answers we can give to even these simple questions are spotty. I couldn't come up with a full dozen answers for my own children. Most kids have trouble coming up with answers even about themselves. Nonetheless, this is a place to start.

Perhaps Jonah is interested in soccer and baseball, does skateboard tricks with his friends after school, wants to be an astronaut, and loves *Mad* magazine. A book like Martyn Godfrey's *Can You Teach Me to Pick My Nose?* would be perfect. It's funny, a quick read, and about skateboarding. A trip to the library could yield a few non-fiction books on space flight and astronomy, two joke books, and a collection of Far Side cartoons. Here's enough reading to keep both of you involved for two or three weeks, and to re-establish your involvement and your enjoyment of reading together. Once you know what works, you can use a reference book like the *Bloomsbury Good Reading Guide* to find other, similar books for your child. Or you can broaden the pick to include books you'll enjoy more, or topics that weren't so obvious on the first run.

Unfortunately, there are some problems with plugging entirely to a child's interests. For one thing, you'll eventually run out of books. I've heard many parents say, "My son will only read books about baseball" or "My daughter spends all her time reading about horses. She's read every Black Stallion books five times." I would caution that books about baseball, or horses, or space flight are only the beginning of wider reading. Children are much more complex than a simple list of interests and activities. As a parent, you should promote books that appeal to deeper aspects of your child's personality – as many books will – and make sure more such books are around the house. My youngest son enjoys soccer, Nintendo, and bicycling, but none of these interests explains his fondness for Bruce Coville's *My Teacher is an Alien* or Brian Doyle's *Angel Square*. Children have complex personalities. Once they begin reading again, they will find that many different kinds of books are of interest.

Teenagers are sometimes reluctant to reveal what really matters to them. If you ask Jennifer for a list of her interests and activities, she'll give you one of those bored looks and announce, "I'm not interested in anything." Of course, the truth is that she spent the previous day worried about everything from hairstyles to existential identity, from Motley Crue to birth control. You will probably have more success with teenagers if you pick a young adult novel you enjoy, say, Robert Cormier's *The Bumblebee Flies Anyway*, then simply announce that you like the book and want to read some of it with them. Sometimes the reading will hook, sometimes not, but discussion at the end of the reading will reveal clearly whether to go ahead or to try a different book.

Using Friends

An important way to build enthusiasm for books and reading is to find a social context for what's read. Your child probably has a group of three or four close friends and perhaps a dozen kids he sometimes hangs around with. Chances are that some of those kids enjoy books. With a little effort – a question to a couple of the kids when they raid your refrigerator, a phone call to their parents – you can find out what's popular with

Matt Christopher: Every Sport There Is

Matt Christopher has written more sports stories than anyone else — some fifty titles now. He might be just the author to hook your bored middle schooler. Try *The Fox Steals Home, Tight End, Face Off*, and *Dirt Bike Runaway* (all Little, Brown) for starters.

TV Tie-Ins for Middle Schoolers

David Macaulay, *Pyramid, Cathedral,* and *Castle* (Houghton Mifflin, 1975, etc.) have been filmed for BBC and PBS.

Lucy Maude Montgomery, *Anne of Green Gables* (McClelland & Stewart, 1908) ties into the video, and musical, and TV series *Anne of Avonlea.*

Robert C. O'Brien, *The Secret of NIMH* (Scholastic, 1971) became a charming Disney animated feature.

E.B. White, *Charlotte's Web* (HarperCollins, 1952) has been turned into a fine animated film, probably available at your library.

Lloyd Alexander, *The Black Cauldron* (Dell, 1965) is actually the second book in a series of junior fantasy novels, but it made an excellent animated feature.

The *Degrassi Junior High* series has a number of accompanying novels, including *Maya, BLT* and *Snake* (all Lorimer). These expand on episodes from the series. The *Degrassi Talks* non-fiction books are even better.

your child's group. Then use that information to provide reading material for your son or daughter.

If your daughter's girlfriends are all reading Ann Martin books, you won't go far wrong if you buy or borrow a couple for her. If the kid next door is hot on Lloyd Alexander sci-fi, use that enthusiasm when you sit down to open the book.

Here's a recent exchange between my youngest son and me, just to give you some idea of the patter involved.

"I was talking to James's mum the other day, and she said that James had just finished reading a great book."

"Yeah?" Alex said.

"It's called *The Indian in the Cupboard,* kind of a mystery, or maybe a fantasy, where this tiny little Indian shows up in a kid's cupboard."

"Yeah?"

"Anyway, I talked to James and he says it's a great book and he couldn't put it down. So I went out and bought you a copy."

The real-life conclusion to this dialogue came when Alex announced that he had already read the book in school a year ago. So I suppose I could have returned the book to the bookstore and used the five dollars to buy something else, but I was already halfway into chapter 2 and I was hooked. Who says kids' books are for kids?

Using Television

For much of this book, I've talked about the importance of setting rules on television watching, and never letting kids view more than three hours a day. But there is an upside to TV that can't be ignored – the tube is a motivator with real force.

Television tie-ins for books provide an immediate social context for what otherwise might be the lonely act of reading. Many shows for young children, from *Polka Dot Door* to *Romper Room* to *Reading Rainbow,* have a book segment in which a picture book is read. If your child seems interested in the segment, a simple question like, "Would you be interested in getting that book from the library?" will give you many titles to seek out on your bi-weekly visit.

Of course, readers at the picture book stage are rarely bored. Our problem readers are older, aged ten and up, and the TV tie-ins for them are more likely to be full-length videos or established series. The *Degrassi Junior High* series, now in reruns, has a series of novels suitable for middle school kids and a number of truly excellent nonfiction spin-off books on teenage problems. The current slew of TV movies based on Lucy Maude Montgomery's *Anne of Green Gables* books will make those characters highly visual for readers who have trouble "seeing" through print. For older teenagers, movies like *Field of Dreams* can provoke an interest to read W.P. Kinsella's novel, *Shoeless Joe*.

The most important action for the parent here is the follow-through. Many books worth reading are suggested by television and videos, but those books will be read only if you follow through with a trip to the bookstore or library. And those books might be read cover to cover only if you give up your time, once a day, to read or discuss the book with your child.

Not Just Novels

Many parents despair that their kids are bored with reading in grade seven or eight because they have stopped reading the reams of fiction that middle school children plough through. Yet sometimes the reading has simply changed form. While I think imaginative reading – novels, short stories, fables – should always be part of the reading smorgasbord, I can understand that some children might use early adolescence as a time to start feasting on magazines and nonfiction for a while.

There's nothing wrong with that.

Ten Great Movies Tie to Ten Great Books for Teens

The Colour Purple. The novel is by Alice Walker (Pocket, 1982); the film stars Whoopi Goldberg.

Blade Runner. The film, starring Harrison Ford, is based on Philip K. Dick's sci-fi novel *Do Androids Dream of Electric Sheep?* (Ballantine, 1982).

Field of Dreams. The popular baseball film with Kevin Costner is based on W.P. Kinsella's *Shoeless Joe* (Ballantine, 1982).

Lord of the Rings. The animated film is by Ralph Bakshi. It's based on J.R.R. Tolkien's trilogy (Unwin, 1954).

Marathon Man. William Goldman did the script and wrote the novel (Dell, 1979). In the film, Dustin Hoffman suffers from the dental drill of Sir Laurence Olivier.

Misery. The Stephen King novel (Signet, 1987) about a kidnapped novelist became a Stephen King film. Quite witty and not nearly as gruesome as *The Shining*.

Presumed Innocent. Scott Turow's best-selling first novel (Warner, 1987) became a solid film starring Harrison Ford.

The Prince of Tides. Barbra Streisand cleaned up the much grittier and harder-hitting novel by Pat Conroy (Bantam, 1986) for the film starring Nick Nolte.

The Silence of the Lambs. Gruesome novel by Thomas Harris (St. Martin's, 1988); gruesome film by Jonathan Demme. Not for the faint-hearted.

Watership Down. A charming novel by Richard Adams (Penguin, 1982) became an animated film with some appeal.

Try Non-Fiction

Many bored readers are turned off by fiction. Try some real-life books:

The Amazing Dirt Book and others in The Amazing series (KidsCan, 1987, etc.), including "milk," "egg," "potato," "paper," and other common items which turn out to be quite amazing. For grades three to five.

Etta Kaner, *Balloon Science* (KidsCan, 1989). A book full of balloon experiments for grades four to six.

Laura Suzuki and David Cook, *David Suzuki Asks . . . "Did You Know"* (General, 1990, 1991). A series of heavily illustrated books about everything in science you ever wondered about. For middle schoolers.

S. Bisel, *The Secrets of Vesuvius* (Random House, 1990). A gorgeous, photo-illustrated book that reads like a magazine on one topic. For grade six and up.

As a parent, you should be encouraging reading and trying to broaden your child's reading interests. But there's no point in disparaging what he actually does read, whether it's a biography of Axl Rose or a weight-lifting magazine from the variety store. Your "bored reader" is at least reading. If you join in by reading a chapter or an article, you'll have a window on the parts of the universe your child is currently exploring. And you'll have something to talk about.

The young boy who reads about motorcycles might be persuaded to read a book like Matt Christopher's *Dirt Bike Racer*. The teenage girl who's reading *Our Bodies, Our Selves* might be interested in looking at Paul Zindel's *My Darling, My Hamburger*. Even if you can't use magazines and non-fiction as an edge to promote fiction, your child is still reading. So long as that's taking place, I refuse to declare *Soap Opera Digest* or *Musclemania* unfit for human intellectual consumption. It sure beats nothin'.

Motivators and Gimmicks

I said at the outset of this chapter that the bored reader needs special motivation – and so far I've suggested you, your time, your child's friends, and the television set. From my point of view, these are the motivators that work consistently to produce long-term changes in behaviour that will build a lifelong reader.

It is here that I differ with many teachers and librarians who will use gimmicks to promote reading. A gimmick is any scheme with short-term rewards for short-term reading improvement. When I began teaching, I used them myself: reading contests with charts on the wall, even free pizza for the five kids who read the most books. Yet none of these contests ever turned a non-reader into a reader. None of them ever resulted in measured reading skill gains that lasted. Even worse, these gimmicks reduced reading to a task, to a kind of work that had to be accomplished to reach some outside reward. This was backwards. Reading should be the reward itself.

Let me be clear: I don't think universal silent reading in school is a gimmick, or giving your child a book allowance, or taking regular trips to the bookstore and library. I don't oppose summer reading clubs at libraries that make reading a social experience, or school book clubs and book fairs, or any of the other wonderful ideas that you'll find in many schools and libraries. But I feel no child should be pushed to read by dangling a pizza slice, or a gold star, or an extra loonie as some external reward for finishing a book.

Getting the bored reader interested in books again requires time, commitment, rules, enthusiasm, and sometimes the purchase of a few books – the same basics when reading began early on. The good news is that improvement can come very quickly, even in a few weeks, if your involvement as a parent is clear.

Two Winners for Kids who Won't Read Anything

Librarians know that when all else fails, every young person will enjoy two books:

Guinness Books of Records (Guinness Publishing), for grade six and up. Then try some of the other "list" books or trivia books available.

Driver's Examination Handbook. The actual name of this publication varies from province to province. It's available free from your local ministry or department of transportation. Guaranteed to catch the interest of boys grade nine and up.

CHAPTER 11

Dealing with the Reluctant Reader

These days, the phrase "reluctant reader" is used by teachers more often than the old term "slow reader," but neither term accurately describes kids with serious reading problems. If your child is a reluctant reader, his problem is not one of reluctance. In fact, your child may be working much harder at learning to read than many of his classmates. His problem is that the act of reading is much more difficult for him than it is for most children.

Both the reluctant reader and the bored reader are likely to turn away from books and fail to keep pace with their classmates. The difference is in the reason why. The bored reader can read perfectly well but lacks the motivation to tackle print. The reluctant reader, on the other hand, has so much difficulty reading that he finds even the attempt embarrassing – or so frustrating that the reading itself lacks any enjoyment. While children frequently become bored readers around grade four and grade nine, the reluctant reader suffers from his problem from early childhood and often throughout life.

The previous chapter talked about bored readers and what a parent can do to spur them on.

A Checklist: Early Warning Signs of a Reluctant Reader

☐ Is your child unable to concentrate or listen to a story for more than a few minutes?

☐ Is he unwilling to read aloud even on a one-to-one basis?

☐ Does he ask assistance of others for decoding easy words?

☐ Does he have difficulty blending phonic pieces to decode long words?

☐ Does he guess wildly at difficult words – or skip over them?

☐ When reading, does he fail to correct misread words that create nonsense?

☐ When reading out loud, does his voice seem flat and disconnected from meaning?

☐ Is his silent reading speed slower than average?

☐ Does he tend to move his lips when silent reading?

If you answer yes to three or more of these questions, consult your child's teacher and/or seek further assessment by a professional.

This chapter will focus on the much more heart-rending problem of the reluctant reader – the one child in twenty who has serious and continuing difficulties with reading. Let's begin with two portraits of two different kinds of reluctant readers.

Mandi A. was born prematurely and developed all her skills slowly. She didn't walk until eighteen months, didn't begin to talk until after her second birthday. By grade three, Mandi was behind her classmates in every subject area. Her printing and handwriting were virtually unreadable. She lost interest in stories read aloud within minutes and had little ability to read by herself. Mandi's grade two teacher suspected problems, but it wasn't until grade three that Mandi's parents agreed to testing by the board of education's psychometrist, a specialist in psychological testing. A three-hour-long intelligence test showed that Mandi's mental abilities were in the low-normal range. Halfway through grade four, Mandi was placed in a special class for children with learning disabilities. In this environment, her reading skills improved, but even now that she is in high school, Mandi's reading remains painfully slow and full of errors in decoding words.

Brandon T. was a bright and active little boy who enjoyed school up until grade three. His math skills developed quickly, and he enjoyed gym and geography, but reading was always a problem. Brandon liked to listen to stories but seemed to have difficulty concentrating on pages of print. Medical tests showed that both his vision and hearing were normal, but his reading skills developed very slowly. By grade five he was significantly behind the rest of his class. A remedial reading teacher began working with Brandon once a week, reviewing phonics, but this had little effect. Brandon's oral reading remained stilted and full of errors. By grade six, Brandon's teacher recommended he be held back a grade, but Brandon's parents refused and asked for a full assessment by the board's psychometrist.

Neither Mandi nor Brandon had problems with motivation or attitude when they began learning to read. They both wanted to read well. Neither of them was going through a family crisis that interfered with their progress in school and reading. Neither was ignored by parents, overlooked by teachers, or left to grow up without books.

Mandi's case is one of "general learning disability" (GLD) – a low level of functioning in many areas that can affect everything from physical co-ordination to higher-level thinking. While Mandi still has the capacity to learn a great deal, her rate of learning and skill development will be quite slow. Mandi will either be in special classes right through school, or, if she is "mainstreamed" in with regular students, will need assistance from a special teacher on a regular basis. Mandi may learn to decode words quite well, but her skills might be limited to "word call," the capacity to read the words without understanding what they mean. Teachers working with Mandi will try to expand her comprehension by enriching her life experience, tying that into books, and working patiently to build her reading skills. If her parents offer similar encouragement at home, Mandi's comprehension skills could develop sufficiently to make reading an important part of her life.

Brandon's problem is more unusual. He's part of that tiny portion of the population that is correctly labelled "dyslexic." To use school language, Brandon has a "specific learning disability" (SLD) in the reading area. He functions quite well in all intellectual and skill areas – except reading.

Children with an SLD are frequently kept in the regular classroom and provided with a special teacher to help them in their area of difficulty. In Brandon's case, no amount of remedial phonics or vocabulary will make much difference. He has to learn to cope with his disability. In senior elementary and high school, a teacher's aide working with the resource teacher will read out

Some Acronyms in Special Education

- GLD: General Learning Disability. This disability suggests problems in many intellectual areas, from reading to math.

- MBD: Minimal Brain Dysfunction was the term used to replace "retarded" but has been superseded by GLD, above.

- SLD: Specific Learning Disability. This indicates that your child may be normal or above average in many areas, but has a problem in one or two specific areas. Real dyslexia is a SLD.

- LDAC: Learning Disability Association of Canada. The parent support group, organized into local chapters.

- IPRC: In Ontario: Identification, Placement, Review Committee. A necessary step before your child can receive a special education program. Other provinces have similar procedures with different initials.

loud to Brandon to compensate for his problem. In high school, Brandon will use audio tapes to help with English reading requirements and tutors to help with other subjects. For English and history, Brandon will do all his written work on a computer with a spellchecker. Brandon's reading skills will likely remain weak, but they can be sufficient to take him through university with extra time and special one-on-one assistance.

What Parents Can Do

If you suspect that your child may be a reluctant reader, it is important to act. Don't let relatives or friends minimize the problem, or suggest it's "just a stage," or use that tried-but-often-untrue line, "He'll grow out of it." No parent wants to panic, but you have every right to seek information and to take action which promotes the welfare of your child.

- Step one: The doctors. You might have an indication that your child is having difficulty in reading or in other areas well before he begins formal school. If so, ask your family doctor to check your child's vision and hearing. A cursory examination in the doctor's office may not be sufficient to diagnose some vision and hearing problems. If either you or your doctor suspect further problems, arrange for additional testing with an ophthamologist (eye doctor) and a hearing specialist. Much early reading instruction, especially in phonics, is based on lessons that must be heard. If your child can't hear the difference between *m* and *n*, he can hardly be expected to read *came* differently from *cane*. Experts note that it is much more difficult to teach reading to deaf children than to blind children.

- Step two: Speak to your child's teacher. Remember that your goal is to ask questions and exchange information. Has the teacher noticed anything about your son that might give a clue to the problem? Does the teacher know of any special interests, or emotional problems, or other factors that might help both of you provide additional support for your child? Have you any observations from home that might make sense of what's happening in school?

  You can't automatically assume that the problems will be simple. Children aren't simply "lazy" or "dumb," nor are teachers simply "boring" or "incompetent." With reluctant readers, the problems are frequently complex, involving biology, genetics, motivation, psychology, intelligence, teaching methods, interpersonal relations at school, and pressures at home. A good teacher can help you understand how some of these might be affecting your child, but only if you are prepared to listen.

  Some parents, unfortunately, are quick to point a finger at teachers and schools, forgetting that four other fingers are pointing back at themselves. If your child seems to be developing a reading problem, be prepared to ask difficult questions of yourselves, as parents, and then act on the answers. Are you expecting too much of your child? Are you providing the home support your child needs? Is your family undergoing a disruption that might be upsetting your child's concentration in school? Are you reading daily with your child? Are you providing a model of the importance of reading by reading yourself?

What the WISC Can Tell You

The Wechsler Intelligence Scale for Children is the most commonly used diagnostic tool for both reluctant readers and the gifted. It yields a broad range of information — much more than just a child's I.Q.

The *verbal subsection* includes defining vocabulary, identifying similarities, understanding oral arithmetic problems, some general information items and reading, and the repeating a set of numbers forwards and backwards. The *performance subsection* involves completing pictures, assembling wooden puzzles, arranging pictures in a logical series, and doing mazes.

A professional can help you analyze the results on individual subtests for a wide-ranging portrait of your child's intellectual strengths and weakness.

- Step three: Testing by school professionals. If you or the teacher feel your child might have a more serious learning problem, it's time to call in the professionals. Most boards or districts employ a number of psychologists, audiologists, speech pathologists, and other specialists. These people can help determine whether your child requires further help.

Usually a school assessment is begun at this time. It looks at your child's school history, his achievement, and his behaviour in different classes. If testing hasn't been done before, your child will take some basic, standardized test like the Canadian Test of Basic Skills or the Gates MacGinite tests. In some provinces, an assessment of this kind can be brought about by requests from either parents or the school. In Ontario, this is called an Identification, Placement, Review Committee (IPRC) and a child is said to be IPRC'd if he is going through the assessment process. Your local board or district of education probably has a pamphlet explaining the procedure for your area.

The next level is a full assessment by a psychometrist (an M.A.-level psychologist who specializes in psychological testing) or psychologist (a Ph.D.-level specialist who does both testing and diagnosis). Such an assessment involves two to three hours of one-on-one testing and interviewing with your child. A full I.Q. test such as the Wechsler Intelligence Scale for Children (WISC) will be administered and a wide range of information can be obtained from that test. Your child may have tremendous ability in some areas and real deficits in others. The board or district psychologist can help you interpret the results and develop a plan that draws on your child's areas of strength and helps improve the areas of weakness.

Unfortunately, the backlog for this kind of elaborate testing is sometimes months long. It is possible, through your doctor or local mental health organization, to arrange for your own testing. But be prepared for fees of up to $500 which are not covered by provincial medical plans.

- Step four: Changing the program. All the testing in the world is useless unless it results in a change in your child's classroom program. The information you've received by this point should result in changes at school, in the classroom, and at home to deal with your child's special needs.

Your child may be served best by moving to a new or special school after the testing is completed. For some problems, especially hearing and vision impairment, there really is little choice. Coming to terms with a disability is difficult for everybody. Moving to a new school or special program doesn't make it any easier, but it is sometimes the best option for your child's future.

Your child may be able to stay in his neighbourhood school and perhaps his own classroom. The board or district professionals will map out a special program for him. This program may involve some time away from regular class (often called "withdrawal"), some special assistance in the school (usually from a "learning resource teacher"), and some changes in curriculum (different reading materials, access to a computer, changes in assignments).

All these changes involve you. You'll be asked to okay any moves that are made for your child, and you'll be asked to help out at home in certain ways. At times

Learning Styles

In 1979, educator Bernice McCarthy began working with McDonald's restaurants to find the most effective way to train employees. She came up with a theory of learning styles, now widely accepted, to show how different people learn best.

- Concrete Experience: These people like real-world problems and situations. "Enough fairy tales, just give me a real book to read."

- Reflective Observation: They need time to understand ideas, and prefer to sit back and watch the teacher and others. "Tell me about the story before I start reading it."

- Abstract Conceptualization: These people need to know the theory behind things; they can apply principles to the immediate situation. "I like phonics."

- Active Experimentation: They like to get right into the work and have little fear of failure. "I like to read three or four things at once."

For a full explanation, see Bernice McCarthy's 4-MAT System.

you'll feel confused and anxious about all this – as if you were at the mercy of all these high-powered professionals. It is often helpful to speak to other parents who have been through this before. Contact your local branch of the Learning Disabilities Association.

Be sure to investigate the new program yourself. Reread Chapter 3 on how to evaluate a school. Ask yourself how *you* would feel in such a school or program. The professionals likely have your child's best interests at heart, but you are still the parent. Don't be bowled over by a conference table of M.A.s and Ph.D.s if you have serious doubts about their recommendations for your child.

What Causes Reading Problems?

The only simple answer to the question is this: we don't know for sure. When you consider the complexity of reading as a skill, it's amazing that such a high percentage of the population becomes readers. But for those 5 percent of our children who have real difficulty with reading, the question *why* is serious indeed. Here's a rundown of the current thinking on the issue:

- Medical approaches. Children who had a difficult birth, who were born very prematurely, or who have problems in intellectual development may often have trouble reading. Some very recent work suggests that medical reading problems may relate to a slowing down in one of the two major visual pathways in the brain. This condition results in a blurred mental image of printed words, like watching a 3-D movie without glasses. Treatment strategies call for oral reading, using computers to lengthen sounds, and visual

Join with Other Parents

The Learning Disabilities Association of Canada is organized into 140 local chapters which bring together parents of all "special" children to share ideas and learn about available treatments. Your phone book will have the local chapter under "Learning Disabilities Association," or contact:

Learning Disabilities Association
of Canada
323 Chapel Street, Suit 200
Ottawa, Ontario K1N 7Z2
(613) 238-5721

The Canadian Council on Exceptional Children is a branch of the Washington-based council. It offers workshops and regular meetings in some cities for teachers and parents. Check with the special education department of your local board or district for more information.

reading through blue filters. But the initial success of these experiments has not yet been backed up by large scale tests.

- Psychological factors. Some children seem to use reading – or the failure to read – as a means of self-punishment, or a way to get back at their parents. This kind of behaviour frequently appears on a short-term basis after parents separate or divorce. But even apparently happy families can harbour deep-seated problems that become visible only in the child's problems in school. The treatment of choice is family counselling with a psychologist or psychiatrist.

- Brain hemisphere dominance. At least one researcher, noting the connection between poor reading and erratic right- and left-handedness, maintains that reading problems stem from the failure of some brains to establish dominance of either the right or left hemispheres. The suggested treatment includes a set of physical exercises to develop co-ordination and "handedness." The effectiveness of all this remains questionable.

- Skill deficits. This approach – big in the fifties and sixties – suggests that reading is made up of a number of definable sub-skills (like phonic blending or consonant recognition) not all of which are mastered by poor readers. Treatment involves careful testing, then drill exercises to improve any weak areas.

- Behavioural reinforcement. Some followers of behavioural psychology see reading difficulties as a problem of motivation. They have suggested techniques that range from electric buzzers to stop sub-vocalizing (moving the lips when reading) to providing candies to readers who

Readability and Reading Difficulty

For proficient readers, a text's reading difficulty doesn't make that much difference in determining whether a book will be read. For beginning readers or reluctant readers, reading difficulty is vitally important. Nothing is more frustrating than a book that is too hard to read.

- "Readability" is a technical measure of reading difficulty. To calculate readability, a teacher will pull three 100-word passages from a book, count syllables and number of sentences, compare vocabulary against standardized lists, then use a chart or formula to calculate the reading level. This figure, say 5.5, means that the average reader halfway through grade five would be able to read the text with reasonable comprehension. Ask your child's teacher for a Fry graph and you can calculate readability yourself.

- "Reading difficulty" involves still more factors that affect reading: size of type, space between lines, whether margins are justified (straight) or ragged, whether there are headings or subheadings, how unfamiliar words are brought in, how sentences are constructed, and whether there are pictures or illustrations.

attain a certain reading speed. While short-term results seem good, long-term improvement in reading is unproven.

- Organizational problems. A very popular approach in the United States these days is to assume that poor readers have trouble organizing their thought patterns. Practitioners feel they help children read better by developing their logic and organization. They use everything from the Mastermind board game to flow-chart idea organizers. The jury is still out on whether there's a spill-over from such activities into reading comprehension.

- Mechanical approaches. This theory, largely discredited now, held that poor readers read slowly because they had too many eye regressions (going back to reread parts of the text). Treatment had students read with a tachistoscope machine, which kept their eyes moving forward so they couldn't look back at misunderstood words. Recent research indicates that this popular sixties idea was dead wrong. Good readers have *more* eye regressions than poor ones; they just do it all faster.

- Learning styles. Proponents of this relatively recent theory suggest that each person has a specific learning style. The lecture approach may work for me; hands-on may work for you. Failure to receive instruction in the proper form will be a stumbling block for some students in reading and virtually every other subject. Good teachers, these days, try to vary instruction techniques to suit a wide range of students.

- *Caveat emptor* is not a learning theory. It's Latin for "let the buyer beware." Over the eighteen years I've spent studying and teaching reading, I've seen theories and procedures come and go. There are no magic cures for serious reading difficulties – not blue filters, or special glasses, or machines, or eye exercises. You can spend thousands of dollars for after-school tutoring – and achieve some real advances – but only because reading will suddenly have become very important around your house. You can make reading just as important, much more cheaply, by following the three Rs in this book.

What We Do Know

While theories on reading problems continued to be developed and debated, two points seem clear:

- One-to-one support helps poor readers read better.

- More reading makes for better reading.

Ordinary children can be taught fairly adequately in a classroom setting with twenty-five other students, but reluctant readers frequently need one-on-one help. There are various ways this can be accomplished at school. At home, the commitment must be yours. Someone must sit down with your reluctant reader and, at an early age, reinforce the phonics and word attack skills while reading your child's favourite books. Someone must listen, later on, as your child begins to read for himself. Someone must be there, later still, to applaud silent reading and to talk about the ideas in what's read. Older brothers and sisters, grandparents, and sometimes babysitters can do all this. But the person to organize a home reading time – and the most important person to follow through with it – is you.

A good school will try to match your effort with similar one-on-one support. Tutors, or education assistants, are trained to help special students on an individualized basis. Reading buddies are

Matching Books with Reluctant Readers

To avoid frustration, a book for a child with reading difficulties should have a readability level roughly equal to the child's tested reading ability. Thus, a grade eight boy, whose reading ability tests at level 4.3 will have little trouble with *Rumble Fish*, which averages level 4.5, but a lot of trouble reading Robertson Davies' *The Manticore*. That's the reason it's important for teachers to know the reading ability of their students and the readability of the books used, not just for reading, but in every subject.

Best Books for Reluctant Readers

Unfortunately, the best books for reluctant readers are hard to find in bookstores because they come from educational as opposed to trade divisions of publishers. Still, your school should have these on hand:

Series Canada (Maxwell Macmillan). A series of high-interest, easy-reading books written at the grade three/four reading level but suitable for students from grade five up. Thirty titles. Some of the best:

> William Bell, *Metal Head*
>
> Martyn Godfrey, *Ice Hawk, The Beast, Fire! Fire!, Spin Out*
>
> Paul Kropp, *Dirt Bike, Head Lock, Amy's Wish, Tough Stuff*
>
> Sylvia McNicoll, *Jump Start*

Series 2000 (Maxwell Macmillan). A series of short novels written at the grade five reading level but suitable for students at grade seven and up. Twenty titles. Some of the best:

> Lesley Choyce, *Hungry Lizards*
>
> Marilyn Halvorson, *Bull Rider*
>
> John Ibbitson, *The Big Story, Starcrosser*
>
> Martyn Godfrey, *More Than Weird, The Last War*
>
> Paul Kropp, *Death Ride, Baby Blues, Not Only Me*

older students or volunteers who try to do the same, but less formally. Both tutors and reading buddies will read out loud with your child, help with written assignments, and sometimes write up stories from your child's own experience – a kind of highly personalized reading program. With this kind of assistance, your child will likely find a success in school that had eluded him before his problems were understood.

The final proven component of any remedial reading program should come as no surprise. It's reading. Nothing improves reading ability like the act of reading. One study compared the results of a dozen remedial programs from phonic drills to comprehension cards to behavioural reinforcement systems. The study concluded that the best gains were made when reluctant readers were allowed to choose books they *could* read and then actually did read. It makes sense. If you wanted your child to learn to swim, you could discuss arm movements, look at charts, and consider the theories of buoyancy. Or you could get in the water and help your child to float. The best way to learn to swim requires getting into the pool. The best way to improve reading requires getting started in the right kind of book.

Books for the Reluctant Reader

There are two basic principles in finding books for a reluctant reader. First, they should be within the range of the child's reading ability. Many of the books suggested on my "must-have" lists in Chapters 4 to 8 will work well with reluctant readers, especially if you help with the reading.

Second, because motivation is so important, the books must be "age-appropriate." Your thirteen-year-old son might be reading at a grade three level, but that doesn't mean he would willingly read grade three books. Special novels like those in Series Canada are a much better choice. These are books written for a teenage audience, but with vocabulary and sentence length controlled so they can be read by students with grade three or grade four skills.

We know, too, that reluctant readers are easily discouraged by books that are technically too difficult. If you can't be present to provide reading support, the reading level of the book must be within the range of your child's abilities. You can't insult your child with "baby books," but at the same time you can't demand that he read a Robertson Davies novel by himself. Check with your child's teacher or the school librarian – and with your child – to find books that will suit.

Many novels are now available on tape, including books for reluctant readers. I have mixed feelings on the idea of "reading along with the tape" for beginning and reluctant readers, because I don't think it encourages the proper attitude for independent reading. However, most of my colleagues in the field feel that audio tapes are a reasonable substitute for an adult reader or reading buddy. Certainly they are better than struggling through a difficult book without any help. You and your child will have to make your own judgement on this issue.

Your Child Can Succeed

Nothing is more frustrating than working with your own learning disabled child – and nothing is more rewarding than when progress is made. Parents will suffer a natural swing from hope to despair and back again that is literally exhausting. But your child's long-term success requires you to persevere. Here, an organization like the Learning Disabilities Association of Canada can help. A chance to meet with other parents once a month to share anger and irritation, achievement, and breakthroughs will help you keep a proper balance at home.

It is never too late to reach a reluctant reader – but it involves commitment and co-operation. Some years ago, I worked with a young man

Mainstream Novels for Reluctant Adolescent Readers

Some novels that work well for ordinary readers will also fly with reluctant readers. Here are some choices:

Anon., *Go Ask Alice* (Avon, 1968). An account of drug abuse and despair which appeals to teenage girls.

Judy Blume, *Tiger Eyes* (Dell, 1981). A teenage girl recovers from the murder of her father.

William Blinn, *Brian's Song* (Bantam, 1983). Based on the relationship between football players Brian Piccolo and Gale Sayers.

S.E. Hinton, *Rumble Fish* (Dell, 1975). Better than *The Outsiders* and technically easier to read. The story of two brothers, one mixed up in a gang.

Robert C. O'Brien, *Z for Zachariah* (Maxwell Macmillan, 1975). Sci-fi survival after a nuclear holocaust.

See also the sidebars for Chapter 10.

Reluctant Readers
Can Read Difficult Books

Some factors can make it possible for a reluctant reader to read even a difficult text:

- Motivation. An interested or motivated reader can read up to four grades higher than tested.

- Pre-reading. A teacher can make a difficult text more accessible by teaching key vocabulary and ideas beforehand.

- Assisted reading. Having a parent or reading buddy to assist with difficult words or concepts can make it possible to read three or more grades higher than tested.

- Independent reading. If your child is going to be reading a book without assistance, keep it at his reading level or below. Recreational reading should be easy, not work. Have your child read a passage out loud and you'll have some idea if the book suits.

named Don over a three-year period from grade ten to grade twelve. Don had come to Ontario from Newfoundland and been in various special education programs before reaching our high school. He had never developed reading skills or much interest in reading. He had good language skills – a real gift of gab, or blarney, if you like – but he couldn't and didn't read.

I tested him in grade ten and the results were dismal: grade three skills across the board. Then, in the middle of that year, Don decided that he wanted to become a priest. He was afraid that with his low-level skills, no Catholic order would take him in – so he found a motivation to read that had been missing before.

I put together a reading program at school that used simple novels like those in Series Canada and a variation on basal readers for skill building. Don enjoyed machinery, so at lunch time I had him work with a tachistoscope to bring his reading speed up from his snail's pace of sixty words per minute. And I called Don's mother, who didn't read well enough herself to help him much, but who was willing to listen to him every night for twenty minutes or so.

By the end of that year, Don's tested reading skills were up to the grade five level and he was on to novels like *Rumble Fish* by S.E. Hinson, and print material from the newspaper. By the end of the next year, Don's reading speed on the machine broke 200 words per minute, his Stanford test showed grade eight skills, and he was reading Paul Zindel's *The Pigman* and William Golding's *Lord of the Flies*.

The following year, Don made it into a seminary. With motivation, reading at home, and an individualized program at school, he compressed five years of normal school progress into two and a half years of real effort.

Your reluctant reader can do the same, at the right time, if you and the teachers are there to help.

CHAPTER 12

Nurturing the Gifted Reader

"Thank God I've only got one of these," said the father of a gifted teenager in one of my creative writing classes. Adam's parents are teachers and are both intelligent, but they have had to work hard for their achievements. Adam's older brother and sister are bright but not exceptional in ability. And then there's Adam.

Adam showed all the early signs of being gifted. He was walking at seven months, reading Dr. Seuss by two, breezing through *Maclean's* by five. He began tackling high school math in grade four and university math by grade seven. His cello-playing began at age four and led to public performances as a soloist at age ten. Adam's accomplishments are impressive, sometimes even astounding. As a child, his party trick was to calculate dates forward, in his head, to tell you that March 15, 2013 will be a Friday.

But Adam's personal life is much more difficult. As a teenager, he has few friends and has never had a girlfriend. His quick and sometimes caustic sense of humour alienates his classmates and teachers. He spends more time communicating through his computer modem than he does talking to any living person. His teachers

Is Your Child Gifted?

Here are a dozen characteristics of gifted children.

- Extremely curious

- Pursues personal interests

- Very aware of surroundings

- Critical of self and others

- Witty; enjoys word play

- Sensitive to injustice

- Questions statements and ideas

- Understands general principles quickly

- Enjoys creative work

- Hates rote-learning

- Sees relationships among diverse ideas

- Generates ideas quickly.

describe Adam as lonely, frequently depressed, demanding to the point of being obnoxious, and below average in emotional stability.

Adam is quite gifted, of course, and has considerable potential to become a highly successful adult. But he is also a child at risk, always in danger of emotional upset, always facing the possibility that he will be marginalized by abuse of drugs, relationships, or his own intellectual intensity. His parents want to nurture his gifts, to help him reach and make use of his potential. To do that, they must obviously support his cello playing and his interest in computers. But they must also help Adam balance his life with reading that is far wider than the fantasy and sci-fi novels he polishes off each night.

Raising a gifted child can be as exhausting as raising a child who is learning disabled. No wonder both these "exceptionalities" are lumped together in school special education programs. Both demand a degree of parental involvement that just isn't necessary with normal children. Both require a special effort on your part to maintain a childhood that is balanced, challenging – but not frustrating – and emotionally satisfying. Books and reading can play an important part in helping you with all this.

Is Your Child Gifted?

If your child is gifted, evidence of it will begin appearing early, even before school age. Look for these characteristics:

- Curiosity. All young children are curious, but gifted children are especially so. Every child wants to know that a particular funny-looking bug is a dragonfly. A gifted child wants to know why it is called a dragonfly if there never were any dragons, why it has four wings instead of two and why it exists at all.

- Intensity. Gifted children are also marked by the intensity of their concentration on a task or idea. Virtually all young children enjoy playing with Lego blocks. But a gifted child will miss lunch to finish a special six-wheeled moon vehicle of her own design. Many bright young people will be interested in space or cars or Barbie dolls. A gifted child can get hung up on a topic for months, collecting books and pictures, building exhibits and doing experiments.

- Ability. Most gifted children start reading and talking at an early age. Some have very special talents and interests. These often appear without prompting by parents. A gifted musician needs her parents' help so she can get her hands on a violin. But after discovering the instrument, she'll want to play the violin herself and will do so for hours at a time.

By the time your child is in second or third grade, her school can provide some additional testing and observation to make the "gifted" label official. This is what the school will look for:

- General Intelligence. By giving your child a Wechsler intelligence test or similar instrument, a psychologist or psychometrist can measure her level of general intelligence (see the marginal note in Chapter 11). One common measure is I.Q., a term developed by the French psychologist Alfred Binet, who used standardized tests to measure a child's mental age, then divided the results by actual age and multiplied by 100 to arrive at an "intelligence quotient." A child who scores with normal twelve-year-olds at the age of ten, for instance, has an I.Q. of 120 ($12 \div 10 \times 100$). Such a child is bright, but

Magazines for the Gifted

Here are some favourites with gifted students:

Prism. Calls itself "the magazine for creative and talented young people." Different themes each issue. For a sample, write:

Prism
2455 E. Sunrise Blvd.
Ft. Lauderdale, Florida 33304

Creative Kids. Publishes works by gifted children, for gifted children. Write:

Creative Kids
P.O. Box 637
Holmes, Pennsylvania 19043

Scientific American. Cutting-edge research; the first few paragraphs of articles are rewritten to be intelligible to everyone; the rest is still fascinating.

Equinox. Quirky Canadian naturalist magazine with some of the best reporting on environmental issues. Some beautiful photography too, like *National Geographic.*

OMNI. A rather low-rent science magazine which appeals to gifted teens.

Maclean's. Canada's national news magazine is essential reading for involved gifted students who may do debating or public speaking.

does not need a special program. About 3 percent of the population has an I.Q. of 130 and above. This level is usually required for a "gifted" designation in schools.

- Creativity. The problem with I.Q. tests is that they best measure certain kinds of thinking, sometimes called "linear" intelligence. Creativity tests like the Torrance Tests of Creative Thinking (Ginn) measure "divergent" thinking, which may apply to more creative activities. For instance, your child might be shown a picture of a stuffed toy and asked to suggest changes that would make the toy more fun to play with. The phrase "gifted" is used for a child with wide-ranging high intelligence. The phrase "talented" is more accurate for a child who has special ability in a single area, perhaps in art or music. In school programs, gifted and talented students are usually combined into a single group.

- Observation. Experienced teachers have taught hundreds of children. Their day-to-day observations of your child's interests and abilities are an important indicator of whether your child would profit from a gifted program.

- Personal and peer evaluation. A gifted child frequently knows that she is "different," as do the other children in the classroom. One study found that three out of four gifted students could be identified by "self or peer nomination."

Your Child Is Gifted – Now What?

You always had a hunch your child was gifted. She began reading for herself long before school and began asking for definitions of words you had to look up when still in the primary grades. She pesters you frequently for new things to do, but once spent two months studying everything she could find about ancient Egypt. Your neighbours think her marks and her achievements are quite remarkable, but you know the truth. Gifted children are frequently tough to live with.

Boredom is the greatest problem. Your gifted child likely taught herself to read. Now she demands new books constantly. If she suddenly becomes interested in knights in armour, she'll want every book on the subject at your local library, then she'll want a trip to the big library downtown. And when she's run out of things to read, she'll start pestering you for other ideas: projects to start, places to write to, things to do. Dealing with all this can be exhausting and expensive, but it can also be wonderfully exciting if you have the time and energy to give to your child.

Social problems are frequently number two on the problem list because a gifted child may feel quite isolated. Her interests are too obscure, or too intense, or too mature for the kids next door. She wants to spend time with older kids or adults, who may not relish time with a very questioning child. As a parent, you want her to have a normal childhood, playing normal games with normal kids, but sometimes this just doesn't happen.

Maintaining a normal life for a gifted child requires a special effort. If your child is gifted in music and busy practising piano two hours or more a day, you'll have to put a special push behind more ordinary activities. Gifted young pianists who do nothing but play the piano rarely make it beyond the first one or two international competitions. They have not developed the personal breadth to connect their playing with life and emotions. Your gifted child deserves more. She needs a whole universe of books to learn about the aspects of life she hasn't time to explore herself. She needs to take time out from her gift so she can play hockey, or learn to use a

Gift Books for the Gifted

Gifted children read so much that it's silly to devise a "must-have" list. Instead, here is a bunch of highly arbitrary gift ideas for that special kid.

- Age seven or thereabouts: David Macaulay, *Castle* or *Cathedral* (Houghton Mifflin). *Mad Magazine* special issues and books.

- Age eight: David Macaulay, *The Way Things Work* (Palladin, 1974). John Fitzgerald, *The Great Brain* (Dell, 1967).

- Age nine: *Calvin and Hobbes* cartoon books. Madeleine L'Engle, *A Wrinkle in Time* (Dell, 1972). Lois Duncan, *Killing Mr. Griffin* (Dell, 1978).

- Age ten: J.R.R. Tolkien, *The Hobbit* (Ballantine, 1937). Ray Bradbury, *Fahrenheit 451* (Pocket, 1967). Katherine Paterson, *Jacob Have I Loved* (Harper-Collins, 1980).

- Age eleven: J.R.R. Tolkien, *The Lord of the Rings* (Unwin, 1954). William Bell, *Forbidden City* (Stoddart, 1990).

- Age twelve: J.D. Salinger, *Franny and Zooey, The Catcher in the Rye* (Little, Brown, 1955, 1945). Various sci-fi fantasy (see Chapter 9).

- And all the books ordinary kids are reading – especially your child's friends.

handsaw, or jump rope with her friends. She needs you to ensure that there is some balance in her life.

However intellectually dazzling a gifted child may be, she is still a child. A mathematical genius or a violin virtuoso may develop the intellect or skills of an adult by age eleven, but emotionally she is still eleven. Your gifted daughter may say she wants to read only Charles Dickens or William Thackeray – especially if this would please you – but she needs to read Robert Munsch, Daniel Pinkwater, and Judy Blume. Your gifted child may prefer to spend time with adults, but she needs the company of children, especially children her own age. Any attempt to short-change the basically slow pace of emotional growth can lead to an adult whose life is lived within an intellectual shell.

If there is a single general piece of advice for the parent of a gifted child, it's this: don't push. Your child is already being pushed enough by her unusual abilities. Your job is to nurture those gifts and help provide balance for her life.

At School: Tough Choices

Your best support in raising a gifted child should be your child's school. Teachers can confirm, counterbalance, and even console you as your child grows. Successful school programs should liberate your child from needless routine assignments and stimulate new interests to be explored. Exactly how these things happen at your child's school depends very much on the policies of your province, the facilities of your school board or district, and the choices you make as a parent.

Thirty years ago, the first choice in dealing with gifted children was acceleration – skipping a grade or two, usually through the elementary years. These days, acceleration is frowned upon. The reasons are simple. Skipping a grade assumes that all skill areas develop equally, and this is true only sometimes. As well, placing a child with older children often limits friendships and models of "age appropriate behaviour." By this, teachers mean that an eleven-year-old with limited interest in sex who has accelerated into high school will either have to withdraw from adolescent hormone-dominated social life, or try to fit in by manufacturing desires and interests that aren't really present. In sophisticated school systems, acceleration is recommended only for children who are emotionally mature, physically large, and perhaps a few months older than their classmates.

When gifted elementary school programs first appeared in the fifties and sixties, they took the form of self-contained classes. Teachers with special education training were placed in classrooms with a somewhat smaller group of students than usual – say, fifteen to twenty kids – rather than the thirty in a regular classroom. The teacher would try to create a program to stimulate all these children as best he could. The children, clustered in their gifted ghetto, often used their intelligence to torment their peers, the teacher, or both. Student refugees from such classrooms have not been highly enthusiastic about the effectiveness of self-contained classes.

The preferred approach these days involves modifying regular classroom programs for gifted students and supplying some special activity on a daily or weekly basis. This approach permits your child to spend most of her time with children of the same age, but to be stimulated by special work both in and out of class. A good teacher can free your child from the rote work that she quickly masters and can challenge her with the special, creative projects that she craves.

As a parent, you should be very closely involved with what's going on at school. Creating a special program is a great idea, but hard for a teacher to organize when teaching a class of twenty or thirty. You are within your rights to expect this for your child – especially if she has been designated as gifted. Speak clearly with the

School Programs for the Gifted

There are a number of school options and opportunities for gifted students. Here's a rundown:

- enrichment in a regular classroom,
- part-time enrichment class,
- full-time ("self-contained") enrichment class,
- extra projects/independent study,
- itinerant teacher/resource teacher,
- special schools
- acceleration (skipping a grade),
- moderate acceleration (three grades in two years),
- special fast-paced courses,
- extracurricular programs,
- mentorship/internship programs,
- special summer courses or camps,
- "Saturday" programs,
- academic fairs or challenges,
- correspondance courses/independent study,
- part-time university credits.

Use Your Community

Many communities have special programs suitable for gifted kids – if their parents sign them up.

- Local museums and art galleries. Most have some sort of outreach program to involve kids. In Montreal, for instance, the Musée des beaux-arts offers classes in art-media from acrylic to watercolour for children.

- Universities. Some universities offer special programs for high school students on weekends, or make their computer or sports facilities available to families for a small fee.

- Forts, pioneer villages, and other tourist attractions. Check for special Saturday/Sunday workshops, March break programs or summer activities.

- Royal Conservatory of Music. In various centres around the country, the Royal Conservatory offers programs not just in playing instruments, but also in dramatics, public speaking, and music theory.

- Community language programs. Your child can study Lithuanian on Saturdays in Edmonton; Icelandic in Winnipeg. Check with your local board or district of education or appropriate community centre.

teacher and principal if you see signs that your child is becoming bored with school.

While the combination of special outside activities and a modified classroom program seems to work reasonably well through elementary school, by high school, students begin to balk at taking on an extra workload. It is here that a large high school with special "enriched" classes can provide the intellectual challenge a gifted teenager demands. Failing this, you can look into special programs and summer camps for your teenager: the Canadian Young Authors' Camp in Haliburton, or the Science Centre Summer Program in Toronto, or the Jeunesse Musicale Music Camp in Quebec. Your school's guidance office should be able to provide a number of possibilities in your area. Or check with other parents in your local chapter of the Association for Bright Children (ABC).

At Home – Reading for Balance

One of the joys that many gifted children experience is their ability to read early and to appreciate very adult material. An ordinary seven-year-old will be just getting out of Dr. Seuss and into short "chapter books". A gifted seven-year-old might well enjoy Ray Bradbury or Douglas Adams, and probably will not need much help to read the books herself. As a parent, you'll enjoy being able to read such sophisticated fare to your child. You'll be able to listen to Sue Grafton mysteries on tape as you drive. You'll find yourself talking about Isaac Asimov, or telescopes, or bits of Greek mythology almost as if your child were an adult.

But you mustn't forget that your child is still a child. Your gifted child may well groan when you say you want to read *The Wind in the Willows,* or she may tell you that she's read it before, twice. But your reading of the book keeps a balance in her life. It tells her that it's okay to be the child she really is.

I've taught gifted teenagers for a number of years, and I'm always amazed at the number of these kids who go back at age seventeen or eighteen to read the childhood classics. These teenagers feel that they missed a stage growing up, and they recapture it through *Abel's Island* or *Alice In Wonderland*. As Joseph Gold, a Waterloo University professor, has termed it, reading can be "bibliotherapy." Books can be used to counterbalance the strains and demands of life. A sheltered child can see great difficulties heroically overcome. A quiet child can read about emotions loudly expressed. Reading is one way to make a gifted child more psychologically whole.

Because of the intensity of their interests, gifted children often want to focus their reading too much. If they get hooked on science-fiction, or fantasy, or computer books, they may not want to read anything else for months or years. Your reading together can provide a leaven. If your son is busy reading only fantasy novels, you should be reading Martyn Godfrey or Gordon Korman with him; if your daughter is on a Spider Robinson kick, better that you read some Judy Blume or Sylvia McNicoll to her. Balance is the key. Your child's teacher or school librarian can help you select the books you need once you've exhausted the choices in this book.

Chances are your gifted child will select her own books at the bookstore or library. Such children can be very pushy about getting exactly what they want. Just remember that you have the power of the wallet. You can use that power to make deals that will balance your child's reading.

Gifted children often prefer to read books written for kids who are three to four years older. By age ten or eleven, many are reading adult books – but adult books of a special kind. The gifted child's intellect makes adult science-fiction, fantasy, and mystery very accessible and quite fascinating. But your child's more normal emotional development makes more subtle literature difficult to understand. That's why Piers Anthony,

- The Ys. The YMCA and YWCA offer more than just swimming programs. Check out their after-school and art programs in your community.

- Etcetera. Toronto has Harbourfront programs in everything from sailing to dance appreciation; artists and teachers in Vancouver offer instruction from batik to dance appreciation; talented music students in Quebec get together under the auspices of Jeunesse musicales to play ensembles. Your community may have special programs offered through 4-H Clubs, or Toastmasters, or Kiwanis. Perhaps a local teacher in your community will teach astronomy on Thursday nights, or a dancer will offer ballet classes on Sunday afternoons. Keep an eye open, or help organize a teaching exchange program to benefit your child.

One Gifted Bookshelf

Courtesy of Jennifer H., now sixteen, of Toronto. The bookshelf over her bed includes, in no particular order:

E.B. White, *Charlotte's Web*

Anthony Burgess, *A Clockwork Orange*

Marilyn Halvorson, *Cowboys Don't Cry*

John Christopher, many titles

William Sleator, *Interstellar Pig*

Stephen King, *The Dead Zone*

J.R.R. Tolkien, *The Hobbit*

Gordon Korman, *No Coins, Please*

Ken Kesey, *One Flew Over the Cuckoo's Nest*

John Wyndham, *The Chrysalids*

Nancy Drew books – five of them

Kevin Major, *Far From Shore*

Robert N. Peck, *A Day No Pigs Would Die*

The Berenstain Bears

Robert Cormier, everything

Frances Burnett, *The Secret Garden*

The Mad Scientist's Club

Claire Mackay, *Minerva Program*

Louisa May Alcott, *Little Men*

Janet Lunn, *The Root Cellar, Double Spell*

George Orwell, *1984, Animal Farm*

S.E. Hinton, *The Outsiders*

Douglas Adams, everything

Betsy Byars, *Summer of the Swans*

C.S. Lewis, the Narnia books

O.R. Melling, *The Druid's Tune*

J.R.R. Tolkien, and Stephen King will work with gifted children, but John Updike and Ernest Hemingway will not.

Reading with gifted children is a joy and a challenge. They love the music of words and the dream that lies behind them, but there's so much more they want to know. A gifted child will sit and be read to for an hour – and demand more. She'll understand every plot twist and demand explanations of words and concepts that an ordinary child would skip over. You'll have to take the time to explain, or admit that you don't understand.

Then you have to follow through. Gifted children flee boredom as other children avoid a bath. You've got to turn the reading into more reading, or into other ideas. Why not rewrite the ending of the book? Why not create your own planet, or fallen empire, or perfect mystery? A clever parent can use reading to stimulate the gifted child's creativity and emotional growth.

Reading To Nurture the Gift

Reading can provide an emotional balance for your gifted child, but it can also be a means for her to explore and extend her gift. A teenager, gifted in science, should have a subscription to *Scientific American*. A gifted young musician will want to read books on ancient instruments, copies of *The Strad*, and biographies of performers. Parents shouldn't have to push this kind of reading, but your gifted child certainly needs a chance to discover it.

Because of the sheer amount that a gifted child can read, almost no family can afford to buy all the books that might interest her. It's important, of course, for your child to own some books that relate to her special abilities, but many more books will have to be begged or borrowed.

The best source is a library. School libraries are often too general to provide many titles on baroque music or great mathematicians. Public libraries can sometimes do better. Many public libraries also do inter-library loans across regions or provinces to bring in books not on their shelves. For the gifted child intently studying insects or the viola da gamba, such borrowing will be essential.

In some areas, university libraries can provide the other great source of books for your child. These libraries frequently keep millions of titles and have subscriptions to cutting-edge research journals and obscure magazines. You can usually arrange special borrowing privileges by accompanying your child to the library, explaining the situation to a library official, and sometimes paying a small fee.

Books related to your child's gift can't be allowed to take over her life. A computer genius still needs to read about much more than computers. But to understand the field that she will likely enter, your gifted child needs access to the field's current research and ideas. With the help of a library or two, you can make sure this reading is available to her.

You're Not Alone

Parents of gifted children sometimes need help. Just like the parents of children with learning disabilities, they may find it easier to cope when they can talk to others in similar situations. Your child's teacher in the gifted program is a good ally and source of advice. There may be an informal group of parents whose children are all in the gifted program. Many cities have a chapter of the Association for Bright Children, which provides a newsletter, conferences, and local meetings for parents to exchange ideas. Check the white pages of your phone book for a telephone number.

Don't try to be everything to your gifted child. You are not teacher, friend, librarian, science adviser, coach, and recital organizer. You are a parent. Seek out the help you need to be the best parent you can. Many gifted children can become very difficult teenagers, some of them in need of

Association for Bright Children

Parenting a gifted child can be trying and lonely. By joining together with other parents, you gain perspective, ideas, enthusiasm, and some clout with school systems.

The Association for Bright Children is an advocacy group seeking better gifted programs in every province. They also offer workshops for parents. For more information:

Association for Bright Children
2 Bloor Street West, Suite 100-156
Toronto, ON, M4W 3E2

professional psychological help. Others need "mentoring," so their gift can be developed by older individuals familiar with the area in which they have special interest or talent. Other gifted children will turn to teachers at school for advice or activities, especially in adolescence. All these people can be helpful to your child and to you in those twin processes of growing up and parenting.

The stereotype of the young genius in glasses, shunned by her classmates, happy only in her home laboratory is the stuff of Hollywood films. Your gifted child can lead an exciting, well-balanced life, using books to extend herself and explore a wide range of interests. Keep reading along with her to stay a part of this.

CHAPTER 13

Reading in Canada: Illiteracy, Aliteracy, and the 21st Century

Reading does not take place in a vacuum. It occurs only when it has purpose, when it is useful, when it brings joy – and when it is connected with power. No child learns to read so he can someday savour a Robertson Davies novel. He learns to read to understand and control the world around him.

Carl Braun of the University of Calgary summed it up nicely when he was president of the International Reading Association: "I believe we need to remind ourselves about the potential of literacy for real *empowerment* – and the obverse, the estrangement, embitterment and the vast human potential that is laid waste as a consequence of illiteracy."

The framers of democracy in France, England, and the United States understood very well the connection between literacy and power. The goal of literacy for everyone stems from democracy's need for involved, knowledgeable, and empowered citizens. No wonder the first act of despots is to seize the mechanisms of print and put limits on personal expression. Yet our society, though we call it free and democratic, is today subject to forces that undermine both literacy and the easy

Adult Readers in Canada

Reading statistics are frequently confusing, conflicting, or flawed, but it is possible to pull together numbers from Statistics Canada, the Southam Report, and the Department of Communications for a quick portrait of ten "typical" Canadians.

- One of the ten can't read well enough to function in our society.

- Three of the ten have limited reading skills and tend to stick to familiar material or what they have to read for work.

- Six of the ten, the literate group, can read well enough to handle a wide range of material. Last week, this group spent four hours reading newspapers, more than two hours reading magazines, and some six hours reading books for work or pleasure. Two of the people in this group didn't read any books for pleasure in the last three months. Two others read about a book a month. Two others read almost a book a week.

- Two of the ten went to a bookstore or library in the past week.

access to books that should be a hallmark of civilization. As we enter the twenty-first century, I sometimes fear that reading – the goal of universal literacy – is in real danger unless all of us rally to defend it.

For the past 500 years, up until at least the 1960s, the progress of civilization has been accompanied by increasing levels of literacy. In most of Western Europe, for example, reading skills expanded from the clergy and aristocracy in the sixteenth century to include perhaps half the working class in the eighteenth century, to near-universal literacy (defined as the ability to sign one's name) by the end of the nineteenth century.

Unfortunately, the historical progress of literacy has been stalled in Canada and the United States since the 1960s. While basic decoding skills are stronger than ever and we now have a larger potential pool of readers, the actual percentage of adults reading is static or in decline. Serious literature and poetry are increasingly unread or connected more to academia than ordinary life. Even the newspaper, that emblem of revolutionary democracy for 200 years, is facing declining readership with its greatest losses among the young.

Some of the decline in adult reading can be explained by our shrinking leisure time and the competition of films, videos, and television for the hours that remain. But I fear a more insidious cause – the entrenching of our current power structure and the despair of many who feel that nothing can be done to change it.

Literacy has always been a means to acquire power for those who haven't yet achieved it – the emerging middle class in the eighteenth century, immigrant groups in the nineteenth century, a wide assortment of groups and individuals in our century. For this reason, universal literacy was seen as a danger to established elites. In the words of one English pamphleteer: "Of all the foolish inventions and new-fangled devices to ruin the country, that of teaching the poor to read is the very worst." Reading, books, and literacy managed to put many more hands on the levers of power – until recently.

While I am not about to suggest that there is an active conspiracy against reading and the empowerment of full literacy, certainly something has happened to stall the progress of literacy in our time. As parents, we want our children to grow up to be literate, active, committed adults – to live better, richer lives than ours. Not every economic and political force in Canada has similar goals.

Illiteracy

We all like to think that Canada is a literate country, that everyone is outfitted with the skills he or she needs to read a newspaper or fill out an income tax return. But the truth is much sadder than that:

- Four million Canadians cannot read well enough to understand this book.

- Another eight million Canadians are "aliterate." They have little interest in reading and get little enjoyment from print of any kind.

- Half the Canadians in the Southam survey could not look up a store in the yellow pages.

After hundreds of years of effort, the goal of universal literacy has still not been achieved in Canada. We manage to get children started reading and through most of the basics by grade three, then we collectively look the other way as the grade four slump strands some readers with minimal skill levels, and we merely shake our heads as grade nine boredom maroons others in an aliterate world of television, videos, and Walkmans. It is not until these lost students reach the world of work that we (especially employers) say, "The kid just can't read."

Adult Literacy in Canada

According to a 1991 Statistics Canada study:

- 62 percent of Canadians had sufficient reading skills to deal with everyday tasks.

- 22 percent of Canadians could carry out simple reading in familiar contexts.

- 16 percent of Canadians had skills too limited to deal with most written material.

The truth is that many Canadians *can* read, but they don't read well enough in a society that demands more sophisticated reading skills. The press and Statistics Canada say that we have three, four, or five million illiterates. The figures vary depending on how we define literacy. Is literacy a mastery of phonics skills? Or the ability to read a newspaper? Or the average ability of a class of grade eight kids?

Large-scale measurement of literacy really goes back fifty years to World War II when incoming recruits had to be sorted on the basis of their abilities. One of the tests involved reading short passages of prose and then answering "comprehension" questions set in a multiple-choice format. The results from these tests provided a statistical breakdown of the reading abilities of millions of men in the 1940s. Obviously, those scoring at the low end were much more likely to end up on the front lines than in officer training school, and reading skills have continued to be used as a kind of social filtering system ever since.

The problem with this sort of measurement is that it handles only one kind of literacy: reading and deciphering short passages. It ignores what is sometimes called "functional literacy," the ability to read bus schedules or nutritional information on cereal boxes. And it overlooks "cultural literacy," a background of information that will enhance the reading of Dickens or understanding of how Canada's parliament actually works. As members of the public, we have been so deluged with numbers and expectations about literacy that many of us ignore the real problem.

But there *is* a real problem. Within your family, or near you at work, or in your network of friends, there is at least one adult who is illiterate. I came across that statement during the 1990 International Year of Literacy and scoffed at it. The statistics may say that sixteen percent of Canadians are virtually illiterate, but surely I did not know any.

I was wrong. Some weeks later I wrote a note for our new housekeeper, a delightful woman who not only cleans the house but looks after everything from laundry to houseplants to gardening. My note was pretty simple: "Can we switch next week? Can you come Thursday instead of Tuesday? New vacuum cleaner bags are in the second floor closet."

I'll admit the note was not highly logical, and my printing is a bit rough, but the message was simple. At least, I thought it was simple.

"Paul," my wife said that night, "I think we'd better *talk* to Mrs. B. when we want to change our schedule."

"Why's that?"

"She couldn't read your note," Gale explained. "First she tried to call her daughter –"

"What?"

"She tried to call her daughter to help her read it, but there was no answer, so she called me at work."

"You're kidding."

"And I didn't know what the note was about, so I asked her to read it over the phone. I thought that maybe you weren't very clear and it needed explaining. But it wasn't what you wrote. It's that Mrs. B. can't read. She got some of the words, but others she had to spell out to me. She was trying so hard, Paul. She wanted to be sure she got the message right."

Illiteracy isn't a problem that is out there somewhere. It is in your own house, or at your grandmother's, or around the corner. Illiteracy isn't obvious. Those who are afflicted by it have developed coping skills to cover their inability to read. They manage to function in extraordinarily clever ways despite being cut off from the world of print. Yet illiteracy – the inability to read well enough to function in a print-oriented society – remains terribly widespread in Canada. According to the Southam study, based on their measure of functional literacy, illiteracy rates increase going from west to east, from a low of

Where Do Books Stand in Canada?

Video rentals (1990): $1.3 billion

Film revenues (1986): $390 million

Tape/CD/record sales (1988): $390 million

All retail book sales in English (1988): $207 million

Trade book sales in English (1988): $120 million

17 percent in British Columbia to a shocking 44 percent in Newfoundland. According to Statistics Canada, half Canada's illiterates are older than fifty-five, but 6 percent of the young people between age sixteen and twenty-four fall into the illiterate group. We cannot simply pigeon-hole illiteracy as a problem affecting the elderly, immigrants, or the poor. It cuts far more widely through the population. Its toll in human misery is enormous. And its cost to Canadian business and society is estimated at $4 billion a year.

There Are Solutions

Frontier College in Toronto has been ·working seriously on the problem of adult literacy for over a hundred years. Laubach Literacy, based in New Brunswick, has established teaching programs right across the country. Other groups have been working through libraries and evening school classes for decades. Since the 1990 International Year of Literacy, there has been some effort by the federal government at least to co-ordinate the various literacy efforts. Today, one phone call to the national literacy hotline at 1-800-263-0993 will let you know what services are available in your community. Or you can look over the sidebars that accompany these pages for a number of other programs to help adults improve their reading.

Adult literacy programs are very different from the standard school approaches I described earlier in this book. For most adults, learning to read begins as a one-on-one experience with a volunteer tutor. As their skills increase, adult learners are grouped into small classes where they will likely find themselves writing a book about their own experiences, or creating a manual for new Canadians, or tutoring very young children in reading. Adult learners can make remarkable strides in reading very quickly because of their motivation and maturity. Often less than a year in a literacy program is sufficient

Community Literacy Programs

- Your local library. Many local libraries are centres for tutoring programs that pair up adult volunteers with adult learners who want to improve their reading. Such one-on-one private lessons offer an effective and confidential way to master reading skill.

- Local literacy councils. Many communities and some neighbourhoods have a literacy council that offers classes, tutoring, and special programs. These councils have few paid employees but many dedicated volunteers who work with adult learners. Check the yellow pages under "Literacy Courses" or ask at the library.

- Your school board. For adults who can read, but want to read better, many schools offer night classes in Adult Basic Education and English for New Canadians. These courses work best for those already literate but weak in English or those with grade three reading skills who want to improve. Classes are small, but unlike the programs above, lessons are still done in class groupings.

to bring reading skills up to a "functional" level.

Unfortunately, the definition of what we might call "functional" keeps changing.

Aliteracy

The literacy required by your child for the twenty-first century goes far beyond those elementary school skills I called "proficiency" in Chapter 7. True functional literacy today requires at least the skills of a teenage reader. A literate adult must have the ability to deal with difficult and complex documents, from credit card applications to income tax forms. A literate adult must have the capacity to apply his own purposes to the print, to find what's important in that twenty-page memo, or to know where to look in the phone book for the Ministry of Environment. A literate adult should have the ability to analyze what he reads, to question bogus surveys or outrageous claims in advertising. To maintain and develop these skills, an adult must keep on reading.

For the past thirty years, the biggest literacy issue has not been one of declining reading skills, it's been declining reading *attitude*. As leisure time has shrunk and television-watching ballooned, the time available for reading has certainly grown smaller. That's understandable and regrettable, but it's only a symptom not the problem. The real problem, as I see it, is that we are losing the active stance of the reader and replacing it with the passive stance of the viewer.

Bookstore owner Bryan Prince has an exercise that quickly demonstrates what I mean. The next time you sit down to read a book or lengthy article for half an hour, keep a pad and pencil beside your chair. Whenever you stop reading to think, or respond, or even go back and reread a section, put a tick mark on the paper. After thirty minutes, you'll find your pad literally covered with tick marks, because reading is really about responding to print.

Two Big Literacy Organizations

- Frontier College. Pioneering work in literacy education was begun by Frontier College in Toronto back in 1899 when it sent reading tutors to work with miners and railroad work gangs. Frontier College still does all that, but now organizes community-based "reading circles" to promote literacy at all age levels. Contact:

  Read Canada/Frontier College,
  35 Jackes Avenue
  Toronto, Ontario M4T 1E2
  (416) 923-3591

- Laubach Literacy. This is the Canadian arm of the big American literacy organization. They've trained some 9,000 volunteer tutors and have organized 150 Laubach Literacy Councils across Canada. The philosophy is a good one: "Each one teach one." Their method uses traditional skill-centred workbooks — and it does work. Head office:

  Laubach Literacy Councils
  P.O. Box 6548
  Station A
  Saint John, New Brunswick E2L 4R9

Now try the same procedure when you watch a half-hour television show. Whenever you stop viewing to think or respond, put a tick mark on the pad. The results will be very different: a handful of ticks, most often marked during the commercial breaks. The reason for this is fairly simple: television is a medium that controls our time. The more effective a television show or video happens to be, the more it seizes the viewer and draws him into the time span of the program. Even with a VCR controller in hand, we are most unlikely to stop, to take time out, to think, to review, or to question our own responses.

These activities are precisely what make reading so valuable. As readers, we are busy interacting with the words in front of us, but we ultimately have control over our own time. We read enjoyable sections of books two and a half times more slowly than we read boring sections. We frequently stop reading to question, or reread for clarity, or speed-read to get to what we really want. Our stance, as readers, is active.

Our stance as viewers is what Witold Rybcynski calls "staring." We are virtually at the mercy of the screen until permission arrives, via commercials, to turn our attention elsewhere.

Pete Hamill, a New York writer, wrote a provocative article for *Esquire* about television viewing and other kinds of "staring." He describes his visit to a twenty-two-year-old crack cocaine addict in a welfare hotel. He was interviewing her about drugs, prostitution, and her own sad tale of squalor while the woman's two children sat watching television. They ignored both Hamill and their mother, transfixed by the screen.

Hamill walked back to his office, disturbed by the interview, the kids, his own indifference to their situation, and a question. Why does a country like the United States, with only two percent of the world's population, consume sixty-five percent of the world's illicit drugs? "Why do so many millions of Americans of all ages, races, and classes choose to spend all or part of their lives stupefied?"

Hamill found an answer on the street: a homeless man in a doorway, begging, and the *look* on the man's face. "I suddenly remembered the inert postures of the children in that welfare hotel and I thought: *television*."

Hamill's moment of insight is based on no research, no statistics, and no longitudinal studies. But I believe he has seen something very important – the way the passive stance of television viewing is changing our society. No population in history has been entertained twenty-three hours a week. No population has been given the message for more than three hours a day that life should be easy and based on satisfying consumer needs. We are the first such experimental group, and the most obvious result so far is that we read less than we did in the past.

For me, the most insidious result of this experiment is its hidden disempowerment of vast portions of our population. It is tragic to visit, as I have, the young people in the Native communities of northern Manitoba and see that their fashions and much of their world-view have been mass-produced in Toronto, copying Hollywood. These young people dress like the students on *Degrassi Junior High* reruns. They talk about middle-class urban culture as if it was their own. And they can find no place for themselves in the real Canadian north that is theirs. They have been literally disempowered by television because the source of their strength – their Native culture – receives no validation on the television screen.

Perhaps some of this can be overcome by teaching our young people to understand how the visual media affect them, as the proponents of "media literacy" in the schools suggest. Certainly, our children need to understand the commercial forces that shape the images they see and the techniques that make those images so effective. But media literacy comes too late for most children, and it is not sufficient. By the time our young people reach an age when they

The Literacy Hotline

The Federal Literacy Secretariat runs a hotline which serves as a referral service. Anyone can call toll-free to get information on adult literacy programs or classes in their community.

1-800-263-0993

can analytically understand what television is doing to them, they will already have watched 300,000 commercials via the tube. They will already have been sold everything from breakfast cereals to electronic toys through commercials so slick that one fifteen-second "message" frequently costs more than an entire thirty-minute program. At that point, after they have been rendered passive consumers, our media educators will explain how this has been done to them.

A Call for Real Literacy

What our children need is not just media literacy but real literacy. They need to be able to read, to respond to what they read, and to write down their own ideas. Literacy is, after all, a tool for defining, expanding, and seizing power for the self – not for melding the self in some kind of collective mass of consumers.

Literacy, as an goal, is connected to eighteenth-century rationalism, the needs of democracy, and the transfer of power from elites to ordinary people. The visual media, as they currently exist in North America, are connected to presenting images, selling products, and maintaining or enhancing the power of the establishment. Unlike the governments in Europe, which place the needs of public and educational broadcasting first, our governments have encouraged television networks and movie distribution systems that have no higher aim than making money for their owners.

In an ideal world, thoughtful films and television programs would take their place beside books as means of communicating with citizens. Each medium would do what it does best. Books would inspire dreams and explore ideas in detail. Films and television would use the strength of the visual image to make emotional statements and raise awareness of problems.

But ours is not an ideal world; it is increasingly a commercial one. The cost of media production is so incredibly high that many voices and opinions are automatically excluded. While a Canadian publisher can bring out an entire book for $25,000, a half hour of prime time television costs $250,000 or more. A Hollywood feature can hardly be made for less than $10 million and often costs upwards of $40 million. Independent filmmakers who shoot on shoestring budgets have difficulty getting general theatrical distribution, which is virtually controlled by Hollywood studios. Low-budget television programs end up with small viewerships, frequently on limited-audience stations – PBS, educational stations, and cable access channels.

So the images that dominate our visual media are effectively limited to the ones that serve those already with power. It was never the intention of those who control Hollywood movies or network television to have it any other way. Nor have our governments made demands that the visual media fulfil a broader mandate – to educate or inform or otherwise empower the viewer. Our politicians seem quite content with voters who evaluate them on images rather than policies, who see themselves first as consumers and only secondarily as citizens.

Until the visual media change their nature or become far more accessible than they currently are, we must continue to promote books and traditional literacy. Any failure to protect reading dooms the weakest segments of our society to marginalized lives. An American study from 1977 found that fifty-five percent of children in families earning under $10,000 a year were functionally illiterate. I suspect that the rate of reading problems among the poor and disadvantaged hasn't changed much since then – but it must if Canada and the United States are to maintain any role at all in a restructured world. All the media literacy skills in the world won't help your son read a technical manual or your daughter write a letter to her member of Parliament. Our Native people will not be better off

A Manifesto for Literacy:

Here's my dream for a program that might turn Canada into a fully literate country, given ten years' effort:

1. Every Canadian has a right to be able to read – and to have access to reasonably-priced Canadian books, magazines, and newspapers.

2. Every school should have a library – with a trained librarian – which would lend books to kids and their families.

3. Every school should have a yearly book budget for each student at least equivalent to the price of a fancy pair of running shoes.

4. Every town of reasonable size should have a public library – which would also be the town's literacy centre for adults who have trouble reading.

5. Library/literacy centres should be open as long as the local video stores. That means seven days a week, twelve hours a day for much of Canada.

6. Literacy means reading. Therefore, no book, magazine, or newspaper should be taxed. No GST, no provincial sales tax – no tax on ideas.

How do we pay for all this? How about a "literacy" tax: start with ten cents on every video rental and send it directly to public libraries. And if that's not enough, let's tax Gucci loafers, or force government ministers to travel on what remains of VIA rail.

Book Trade Talk

- "House": a publisher. There are some 350 book publishers in Canada with over 1,000 employees, but only 42 houses had sales over the million dollar mark.

- "Product": the books. In 1990, 8,249 titles were published in Canada.

- "Textbooks" and reference books make up about half of publishers' sales.

- "Trade books": the books you find in bookstores. There are roughly 3,000 new titles offered every year in Canada.

- "Mass-market books": paperbacks often found on supermarket and variety store racks. These books are printed so cheaply that, when unsold for three months, the store owner merely rips off the cover and returns it for credit.

- "Independents": bookstores not owned or franchised by a chain. These stores sold some $67 million of books in 1990.

- "Chains": stores like Coles or W.H. Smith. Chain stores account for $107 million in sales.

having learned via television that life might be better in Winnipeg or Toronto, but they might well profit from reading entrepreneurial manuals or writing effective business plans.

At a certain level, parents and teachers know this. Sometimes I think our governments actively look the other way. Book purchases by school boards and districts have been falling for the past fifteen years. They now average slightly more than twenty dollars a year per student, about enough for two softcover books or half a textbook. School library budgets are often the first to be cut when money is tight. Public library budgets have been increasing slightly, but always at a level below the rate of inflation so book purchases decline. The net effect of all this is that fewer books are available for our children.

Which Way for Canada?

While there was much talk in 1990 about our five-year plan for the International Year of Literacy, there was precious little action until quite recently. The federal government pledged $22 million in new funding, but this was spread out over five years and designated specifically for projects to raise public consciousness of literacy concerns. The net effect of this approach can be seen in bus posters, surveys, and pilot programs across the country. But real adult literacy programs are still in the hands of unpaid volunteers, run out of storefronts or library backrooms, dependent on a trickle of government grants and municipal charity. I feel that Canada's four million less-than-literate adults deserve better.

At the same time, Brian Mulroney's government has become the first in Canadian history to tax books and reading. The much-hated GST is the first tax ever levied on books. To make matters worse, some provincial governments have chosen to co-ordinate their sales taxes with the GST. In Quebec and Nova Scotia, this decision has placed taxes of 15 percent and 16 percent on books where there were no taxes before.

Nor has free trade been kind to our publishers. While it is possible, I suppose, that Tree Frog Press might expand from its Edmonton base and somehow get its books into the Doubleday stores on Fifth Avenue, it's probably more likely that all the people in American border states will suddenly begin rushing across the border to shop in Canada.

Our relatively small publishers, working with a population base the size of New York State, are not in a position to take on the full fifty states down below. The financial resources and marketing clout simply aren't there. But a New York publisher can supply all of Canada with an American book by doing a print overrun of 10 percent. Thanks to the free trade agreement, we are powerless to protect ourselves. Those few subsidies that our publishers do enjoy, like the book rate offered for mailing, are now in danger for fear our American partners may find them a restraint on free trade.

"So what?" some might say. "Can't our demand for books be handled out of New York the way our demand for films and videos is handled out of Hollywood?"

Yes, but with tremendous costs for our children. When Canadian authors no longer have Canadian publishers who can print and promote their work, our children will no longer be able to look to books to see a reflection of their lives. Movies and television cannot fill the gap because of the incredible capital costs involved in production. When we see Toronto appear in a film, it is more likely to be disguised with trucked-in garbage to resemble Chicago or some generic American city. Our children know more about Cicely, Alaska, thanks to *Northern Exposure*, than they do about Moose Jaw or Le Pas, despite the best efforts of the CBC. Such cultural disempowerment is beginning to show.

I teach a creative writing class in a Hamilton,

The Cost of a Book: Where Your Twenty Dollars Goes

Cost of book to you: $21.40 or more.

- Tax: $1.40 GST. Sometimes the provincial tax is piggybacked, raising the $20.00 book to $23.00 in Quebec or $23.20 in Newfoundland.

- Bookstore: $8.00. When the store purchases a book from the publisher or wholesaler, it receives a discount that runs from 38 to 48 percent.

- Printing and typesetting: $4.00. Costs vary widely depending on paper quality and the expense of the cover.

- Binding: $1.50. The "perfect" binding used for paperbacks and many hardcover books is basically just glue. The old sewn binding would triple this cost.

- Editorial work: 50 cents. A book usually has a substantive editor who calls for major changes and a copy editor to correct spelling and grammar.

- Publisher overhead: $2.60. Advertising, warehousing, copies to reviewers, salaries for staff.

- Mailing, shipping: $1.00. Canada's cheap "book rate" may be eliminated in the near future.

- Author royalty: $1.60. The standard paperback rate is 8%; hardcover books pay 10% to the author. Most authors receive an "advance" against future royalties, frequently larger than what the book will actually earn.

- Profit: 80 cents. Three out of four books lose money for their publishers.

So You Want To Be A Writer?

Average annual income in 1991 of various professions:

- Major league baseball player: $891,188 (US)

- Ontario high school teacher, highest category and experience: $63,540

- Average Canadian teacher: $45,875

- Canadian magazine writer: $28,500

- Canadian book author: $21,300

(last two figures from a 1985 government study, adjusted for inflation to 1991 levels)

Ontario high school. Last year I asked my student writers to tell me about their stories-in-progress.

"And where's your story set, Jan?"

"Philadelphia."

"Oh. Yours, Graham?"

"Byzantium. The twelfth century."

"Right. And your story, Sara?"

"Could be anyplace, sir."

"I see," I responded, my nationalist gorge beginning to rise. "So we have two stories in Los Angeles, one in Philadelphia, one in Washington, one in Turkey, two in some mythical future kingdom, and a bunch that could be anywhere. Has anyone placed a story here in Canada?'

Blank faces around the circle. One girl lifted her hand.

"Mine's in Owen Sound," she said.

The other students laughed. "Owen Sound!" Sara giggled. "Why would anyone put a story in Owen Sound?"

It was a difficult question and the girl blushed. Her story was based on the life of her grandmother. She thought it was a story worth writing and I certainly agreed.

Our Canadian stories and our personal experiences *are* worth writing. We should never be put in a position where a writer in Saskatchewan has to modify her work so it seems to come from Colorado. But if there is no outlet for the works of Canadian writers – and no Canadian books to fuel the imaginations of our young people – then how will we hold onto our own dreams and histories?

If our various governments continue to permit the book industry to erode, then the only identity left for our children will be the one that dominates the visual media in their lives. If our federal government continues to regard books as just another consumer product, who will protect our publishers against American market dominance? If all our governments continue to add taxes to books while taking away subsidies, how long will it be before Canadian books are ridiculously expensive in comparison to American mass-market paperbacks and ninety-nine-cent video rentals at the milk store?

As parents, we have to speak up to protect books and reading in Canada. While the issues are complex and the measures required hardly simple, we need to develop some national and political will to ensure that books and reading are not sacrificed to conservative economic theories or government cost-cutting.

Beyond the Year 2000

Much of this discussion has focused on the importance of books to children and to Canada. But I suspect that the future is not so much in the book or the printed page, but in print itself.

One of the problems with books is that they are expensive. A hardcover book, historians say, has cost roughly the same as a good dinner out for some 300 years. The only real cost breakthrough in publishing came with the development of the paperback book, with its cheap glued spine and pulp pages. We now have new classes of books, like the one in your hands, that fall halfway between hardcover and mass-market paperbacks. While there have been some attempts to cut the costs of producing a book – the "perfect" binding, computerized typesetting, simultaneous printing of hardcover and trade paperbacks – books remain quite expensive for large portions of the population. For this book to reach the parents of the 840,000 Canadian children in low-income families, it should be cheaper than a pack of cigarettes. But that's impossible with current technology.

While book prices have remained relatively stable, the prices for other kinds of information technology are rapidly shrinking. My family's first television set cost two months of my father's salary. Now a little black-and-white portable costs less than an average day's pay. The cost of renting a videotape at our local store has gone down from $5.99 to $.99 over the past five years. The computer I worked on in high school, which took up two classrooms, can now be replicated in one microscopic dot on one section of a computer chip. Computer memory costs are declining by a factor of 1,000 every five years.

Yet I say that the future is still in print. Probably print on a computer screen, but definitely print.

My step-daughter, a graduate student in psychology, has to read a great deal – and much of that reading is from a computer screen. My older two sons, both in engineering, probably spend as much time studying screens as books. They're all still reading, but the print has moved off paper and onto phosphor or LCD displays.

In a charming and ironic way, the computer has even restored one nineteenth-century skill: letter writing. Most adults of my generation have written perhaps a few hundred letters in our lives. But my children are plugged into computer networks that send and receive electronic mail at a staggering rate. Hundreds of electronic "newsgroups" allow them to read and respond to topics ranging from "alt.humor.funny" to "soc.culture.ukrainian."

All of this still requires reading – often reading at great speed as information scrolls on the screen. It still requires the skills of analysis, response, and interaction that are the touchstones of any real literacy. Computers, ironically, are not making skills in reading and writing any less necessary. They are making them more essential.

In the century to come, I do not fear for literacy, which will certainly survive for the educated elite. My fear is that real literacy will be the preserve of only a few, while many others will lapse into a passivity that saps their economic and political strength. As parents, we can't allow this to happen. Reading – real literacy – should be a birthright for *all* our children.

Notes on Sources

Chapter 1

For a history of reading and language, try Robert McCrum, William Cran, and Robert MacNeil's *The Story of English* (Viking, 1986), or Victor Neubergs's *Literacy and Society* (Woburn, 1971). The strongest proponent of reading out loud to children is a former newsman named Jim Trelease, whose *The New Read-Aloud Handbook* (Penguin, 1982,1989) provides a bibliography of many excellent read-aloud books for young children. Basic principles of encouraging reading can be found in an inexpensive, 1990 booklet by Nancy Roser, *Helping Your Child Become a Reader* (International Reading Association, 800 Barksdale Road, P.O. Box 8139, Newark, Delaware 19714, US$1.75). Much work on the development of reading skills can be found in Jeanne Chall's *Stages of Reading Development* (McGraw Hill, 1983). Alan King's findings are in *The Adolescent Experience* (Ontario Secondary School Teachers' Federation, 60 Mobile Drive, Toronto, Ontario M4P 2Y3, 1986). Caroline Snow's study of parents, families, and reading is called *Unfulfilled*

Expectations: Home and School Influences on Literacy (Harvard University Press, 1990).

Statistics on television-viewing are from Statistics Canada surveys and Barry Duncan's *Mass Media and Popular Culture* (Harcourt Brace Jovanovich, 1988). David Suzuki's VCR idea is from an interview in OSSTF *Forum*. The National Assessment of Educational Progress (NAEP) is ongoing: see *Three national assessments: Changes in performance. 1970-1980* (Denver: Education Commission of the States) and *The Reading Report Card* (Princeton: Educational Testing Service, 1985).

Chapter 2

Two of the best books on reading theory are Jeanne Chall's *Stages of Reading Development* (op. cit.) and Frank Smith's *Understanding Reading* (Holt, Rinehart and Winston, 1978, 1982). The two conflicting theories on reading could be called instructional versus psycholinguistic rather than "phonics" versus "whole language." Jeanne Chall still favours systematic instruction in her *The Reading Crisis: Why Poor Children Fall Behind* (Harvard University Press, 1990), supported by a number of researchers including George Spache in *Good Reading for Poor Readers* (Garrard, 1964, 1966, 1974). Frank Smith is joined with other important psycholinguists including the Goodmans: Kenneth Goodman, *The Psycholinguistic Nature of the Reading Process* (Wayne State, 1968) and Yetta Goodman, ed.; *How Children Construct Literacy* (International Reading Association, 1990), and the Chomskys: Noam Chomsky, *Language and Mind*, (Harcourt Brace Jovanovich, 1968); Carol Chomsky, "Stages in Language Development," *Harvard Educational Review*, 1972, 42, 1–33.

Marilyn Jager Adams' book *Beginning to Read: Thinking and Learning About Print* (MIT Press, 1990) is excellent on reading techniques and technicalities. The strongest argument for simple phonics is still Rudolph Flesch's *Why Johnny Still Can't Read?* (Harper & Row, 1981), the follow-up to his 1955 classic, *Why Johnny Can't Read?* Sylvia Ashton Warner's *Teacher* (Simon and Schuster, 1963) discusses her experiences teaching Maori children. Tololwa Mollel's *The Orphan Boy* is an Oxford University Press (1990) publication, with illustrations by Paul Morin.

Chapter 3

An excellent discussion of what makes a good school can be found in Alan King's *The Good School* (Ontario Secondary School Teachers' Federation, 1988). Jeanne Chall's *The Reading Crisis* (op.cit) offers a good discussion in chapter 7 of effective schooling. The most important book on the effective schools movement is James Slezak's *Odyssey to Excellence* (Merrit, 1984). The first chapter of Hedley Beare, et al, *Creating an Excellent School* (Routledge, 1989) offers a good international overview of the same material. The Scarborough Ontario Board of Education has an excellent pamphlet called "Resolving Parent/School Conflicts" (140 Borough Drive, Scarborough, Ontario M1P 4N6) if you cannot find something similar at your board or district. Wendy Warren, *et al. Teachers and Literacy* (Canadian Teachers' Federation, 110 Argyle Avenue, Ottawa, Ontario K2P 1B4, 1991) was funded by the Literacy Secretariat.

Chapter 4

There is much good advice about reading with young children in Nancy Larrick's *A Parent's Guide to Children's Reading* (Bantam, 1982). Marcia Baghban's study is *Our Daughter Learns to Read and Write* (International Reading Association, 1984). The importance of parental involvement in early reading is supported in many studies including Jodi Grant and Carol Brown's "Precocious readers: A comparative study of early reading" in *Alberta Journal of Educational Research* (September 1986, Vol. 32(3) 223–233) and William F. White's "Perception of home environment and school abilities as predictors of reading power and school achievements" in *Perceptual and Motor Skills*, (June 1986, Vol. 62(3) 819–822). Daniel N. Stern's *Diary of A Baby* (Basic, 1990) is an excellent treatment for the general reader on early childhood development. The questions sidebar is from "Preschooler's Questions about Picture," by David Yaden, Laura Smolkin, and Alice Conlon in *Reading Research Quarterly* (Spring 1989, Vol. 24(2) 188–214).

Chapter 5

For parents of beginning readers, there's much good advice and some excellent reading games in the *Reading Is Fundamental Guide* (Doubleday, 1987) and solid, if all-American, reading lists. The excellent *Reading: A Lifelong Adventure* (1990) is all-Canadian, from the Canadian Children's Book Centre (35 Spadina Road, Toronto, Ontario M5R 2S9). The warning on ruling television is again from research by Caroline Snow. Frank Smith's *Reading Without Nonsense* (New York: Teacher's College Press, 1986) offers solid theory. *Teacher* magazine devoted a whole issue to whole language: *Teacher*, August 1991.

Parents who would like more annotated reading lists to build a children's library can refer to *Choosing Children's Books* by David Booth, Larry Swartz, and Meguido Zola (Pembroke, 1987), which annotates some Canadian titles and is quite good in suggesting books for younger readers. The encyclopaedic *New York Times Guide to the Best Books for Children* by Eden Ross Lipson (Random House, 1991) has synopses of 1,700 children's books. Donald R. Stoll's bibliography *Magazines for Children* (1990) is available from the International Reading Association.

Chapter 6

Again, Jeanne Chall's *Stages of Reading Development* (op.cit) is excellent in describing expectations by grade level. Michele Landsberg's *Guide to Children's Books* (Penguin, 1986) raises the issue of using boredom to further a child's reading and surveys many children's books as well. A book primarily for librarians by Joanne Oppenheim, *et al. Choosing Books for Kids* (Ballantine, 1986) reviews 1200 mostly-American books for children under age twelve.

Chapter 7

Canadian children's literature is discussed at length in Sheila Egoff's *The New Republic of Childhood* (Oxford, 1990). A more valuable guide for parents, though heavily American, is Betsy Hearne's commonsense book *Choosing Books for Children* (Dell, 1981).

Chapter 8

Most of the statistics in this section are from Allen King's *The Adolescent Experience* (op.cit.). Study skills are discussed in *The Reading Edge: Sharpening Reading and Study Skills* by John Gardner, Ted Palmer, and Jack Shallhorn (Ontario Secondary Schools Teachers' Federation, 1987). Speed-reading is handled by many popular books; I like Robert Zorn's *Speed Reading* (HarperCollins, 1991), though he still thinks eye regression is a bad thing. G. Robert Carlsen's *Books and the Teenage Reader* (Bantam, 1967) offers a good general discussion, but is quite out of date now.

Chapter 9

Robert MacNeil's *Wordstruck* (Penguin, 1989) is worth reading just for the language. Mortimer Adler's *How to Read a Book* (Simon & Schuster,

1967,1972) is now a classic. Joseph Gold's *Read For Your Life* (Fitzhenry and Whiteside, 1990) is both intelligent and well written. His discussion of bibliotherapy is quite fascinating. Victor Nell's *Lost in a Book: The Psychology of Reading for Pleasure* (Yale, 1988) is intelligent, but quirky in both its experiments and concepts. Witold Rybcynski's book *Waiting for the Weekend* (Viking, 1991) has much to say on reading and leisure time. Most of the reading statistics can be found in *Reading in Canada 1991* done by Ekos Research (275 Sparks Street, Suite 801, Ottawa, Ontario K1R 7X9) for the Department of Communications. Some additional statistics came directly from Ekos.

Chapter 10

Kenneth McLeish's *Bloomsbury Good Reading Guide* (Bloomsbury, 1988) suggests many teenage and adult books with an interesting approach: look up an author you like and the *Good Reading Guide* will suggest a half-dozen other books you'll probably enjoy. M.H. Zool's *Good Reading Guide to Science Fiction and Fantasy* (Bloomsbury, 1989) does the same for those genres.

Chapter 11

There is still much basic information in George D. Spache's *Diagnosing and Correcting Reading Disabilities* (Allyn & Bacon, 1976) on reading problems and testing procedures. Lee Cronbach's *Essentials of Psychological Testing* (Harper & Row, 1984) is the basic reference volume on testing. Readability in many languages is explained in *Readability: Its Past, Present and Future* edited by Beverly Zakaluk and S.J. Samuels (Newark, Delaware: International Reading Association, 1988). Learning styles can be found explained in Bernice McCarthy's *4-Mat System: Teaching to Learning Styles With Right/Left*

Mode Techniques (Barrington, Illinois: Excel Inc, 1980). Teachers will be interested in the bibliography *Easy Reading* by Randall Ryder, Bonnie and Michael Graves (International Reading Association, 1989).

Chapter 12

A good overview of gifted education around the world is in Kurt Heller's *Identifying and Nurturing the Gifted: An International Perspective* (Hans Huber, 1986). Thomas Southern and Eric Jones have edited *The Academic Acceleration of Gifted Children* (Columbia, 1991), which considers the pros and cons of various programs. For teachers, Jeanette Parker's *Instructional Strategies for Teaching the Gifted* (Allyn & Bacon, 1989) offers many clever, workable ideas. Mildred and Victor Goertzel's *Cradles of Eminence* (Little, Brown, 1962) offers life stories of 400 gifted persons. The best general book for parents is *Your Gifted Child* by Joan Smutney, Kathleen and Stephen Veenker (Oxford, 1989). Canadian programs are outlined in *The Bright and the Gifted* by Fred Speed and David Appleyard (University of Toronto: The Guidance Centre, 1985).

Chapter 13

Illiteracy was brought to everyone's attention by Peter Calamai's Southam press survey, *Broken Words* (Southam Newspaper Group, Suite 900, 150 Bloor Street West, Toronto, Ontario M5S 2Y8). Subsequent statistics are from a 1991 Statistics Canada study and their annual review of Canadian publishing. *Canadian Living* devoted much of their January 1990 issue (pp. 39–53) to an excellent survey of the adult illiteracy problem and the programs available to deal with it. Pete Hamill's article "Crack and the Box" is in *Esquire*, May 1990. School textbook budgets are analyzed in Sandy Greer's "The Battle for Books"

(OSSTF *Forum*, Dec. 86/Jan. 87, 28–32). James Lorimer's study *Book Reading in Canada* (Toronto: Association of Canadian Publishers, 1983) was our first study of reading and publishing in Canada; *Reading in Canada 1991* (op. cit.) is the most recent.

Index